THE EARLIEST AMERICANS

THE EARLIEST AMERICANS

by HELEN RONEY SATTLER

Illustrated by JEAN DAY ZALLINGER

CLARION BOOKS · NEW YORK

ACKNOWLEDGMENTS

I am deeply indebted to many people for their help in writing this book. I especially want to express my deepest appreciation to Dr. James McKenna, chairman, department of anthropology, Pomona College, and to his wife, Dr. Joanne Mack, for reading the completed manuscript and for offering valuable suggestions and bits of important information I would not otherwise have known, as well as for checking the drawings for accuracy. I also want to thank my son, Dr. Richard Sattler, for sharing his knowledge of early American cultures, for providing me with references, and for reading and criticizing the finished manuscript. Finally I want to extend my thanks to Dr. Ed Sieman, University of Pittsburgh, for taking the time from his busy schedule to give me a personally guided tour of the Meadowcroft site and for sharing his knowledge about it.

Clarion Books
a Houghton Mifflin Company imprint
215 Park Avenue South, New York, NY 10003
Text copyright © 1993 by the Estate of Helen Roney Sattler
Illustrations copyright © 1993 by Jean Day Zallinger

Library of Congress Cataloging-in-Publication Data
Sattler, Helen Roney.
The earliest Americans / by Helen Roney Sattler ;
illustrated by Jean Day Zallinger.
p. cm. Summary: Covers the history of early man in America from the earliest known sites to approximately 1492 A.D. ISBN 0-395-54996-5 1. Indians—Origin—Juvenile literature. 2. Paleo-Indians—Juvenile literature. 3. America—Antiquities—Juvenile literature. [1. Indians—Origins. 2. America—Antiquities.] I. Zallinger, Jean, ill. II. Title. E61.S28 1993
970.01′1— dc20
91-9463   CIP   AC

BP 10 9 8 7 6 5 4 3 2 1

Contents

Introduction

THE PEOPLING OF the Americas is one of the most exciting and tantalizing scientific detective stories of the twentieth century. New discoveries of ancient sites, and new tools with which to study both old and new evidence, have provided a wealth of knowledge about the people who first populated the new world and their descendants. Helen Roney Sattler presents a vivid, thorough, and stirring account of what are now thought to be the most likely origins of the earliest Americans, and she ably documents the emergence of cultural diversity in the Americas.

Where did the first migrants come from? How did these preindustrial people manage to travel in Arctic conditions across a 1300-mile-wide land bridge (Beringia), now under the ocean, and then journey on to the southernmost tip of South America at least twenty thousand years before Columbus? Sattler describes in rich detail what these journeys must have been like, based on the most recent studies of the principal archaeological sites.

The heirs of the original Americans went on to construct the magnificent cliff dwellings of Mesa Verde, Colorado, the giant kivas of Chaco Canyon in New Mexico, the pyramids of the Mayas, the mounds of the Mississippi Valley, and the chinampas or "floating gardens" in the Valley of Mexico, and to stand on the shores of Tierra del Fuego, South America, having conquered every environmental obstacle along their way. Sattler presents these accomplishments and more in clear, economical language, revealing what is known from evidence, admirably avoiding the temptation to speculate. Jean Day Zallinger conveys equally valuable information in her meticulously researched and artistically rendered illustrations. With this book, Sattler and Zallinger together have made a significant contribution to an important area of anthropological and archaeological literature.

JAMES J. MCKENNA
Associate Professor of Anthropology
Chair, Department of Sociology
  and Anthropology
Pomona College
Claremont, California

CHAPTER ONE

Where the First Americans Came From

WITH GASPING BREATH and aching legs, I took the last step to the top of the twenty-stories-tall Pyramid of the Sun at Teotihuacán (tay-OH-tih-wah-KAN), just north of Mexico City. This pyramid once served as the platform for a temple. I marveled at the stamina of the priests who, I supposed, must have climbed those steps daily. As I gazed upon the remains of the ancient city that lay below, I wondered about the 150,000 people who lived, worked, and played there more than 2000 years ago. They had planned their city well, laying it out in a perfect grid pattern. This was obviously a center of highly intelligent and civilized people who were accomplished engineers and scientists.

It is estimated that there were 30 or 40 million people — about as many as live in the states of Washington, Oregon, and California today — living on the two continents at the time of Columbus's arrival in 1492. The first European explorers found the Americas inhabited by hundreds of different cultural groups occupying every possible environmental niche and speaking more than a thousand different languages. Who were these people? Where did they come from?

There is widely accepted proof that Columbus was met by people whose ancestors had been on the American continents for at least 15,000 years. It is possible that the very first Americans arrived even earlier. There are many bits and pieces of evidence that lead some scientists to believe in earlier arrival.

Most archaeologists (scientists who study ancient people) believe the first Americans emigrated from northeastern Asia. A Stone Age people called Dyukhtai (named for the Dyukhtai Cave where their artifacts were found) lived in eastern Siberia, and used tools very similar to those used by the first Americans. Physical features of modern Native Americans are similar to those of Siberian people. Both have dark eyes, straight black hair, and ruddy complexions. Also, many Native Americans have distinctive tooth patterns. The only other group of living people with the same kind of tooth pattern, which is called Sinodonty, lives in eastern Asia. Too, the skeletons of Native Americans are quite similar to fossil skeletons of early Siberians. In fact, Siberian fossil skeletons resemble the skeletons of modern Native Americans even more closely than they do the skeletons of present-day Siberians. There are also similarities in the languages of East Asians and Native Americans.

Although most scientists agree that the first Americans origi-

Sinodonty, the tooth pattern that only Native Americans and northern Asians share, includes shoveling (scooped-out surfaces) of the upper incisors (a), single-rooted first premolars (b), and triple-rooted lower first molars (c).

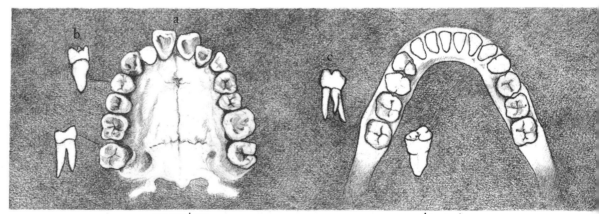

upper jaw   lower jaw

NATIVE AMERICAN TEETH

nated in Asia, they argue a lot about how and when they came. Today Asia is separated from North America by the Bering Strait — fifty-five miles (88.7 kilometers) of shallow but very rough seas. However, there were periods during the history of the earth when people could have walked from Asia to North America. During the Ice Ages so much of earth's water was frozen into continental glaciers (ice sheets) that the sea levels dropped. Each time the level dropped more than 170 feet (fifty meters), the Bering Strait drained and its floor became a dry land bridge connecting the two continents. This land bridge is called Beringia after the Bering Strait.

Most scientists think the first American settlers came over this land bridge and so place the migration at a time when it existed. Even though the first Australians crossed a wider stretch of sea to reach Australia 50,000 years ago, some consider it unlikely that the earliest Americans could have crossed the dangerous waters of the Bering Strait. Eskimos, however, were crossing the Bering Strait to trade with the Siberians long before the arrival of Europeans. They crossed on ice in the winter and may have had boats for summer crossings. Therefore, some scientists see no reason the earliest Americans could not have crossed the same way.

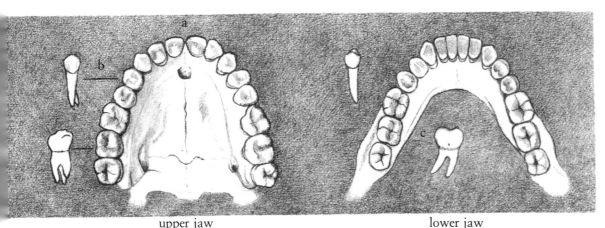

upper jaw   lower jaw

EUROPEAN TEETH

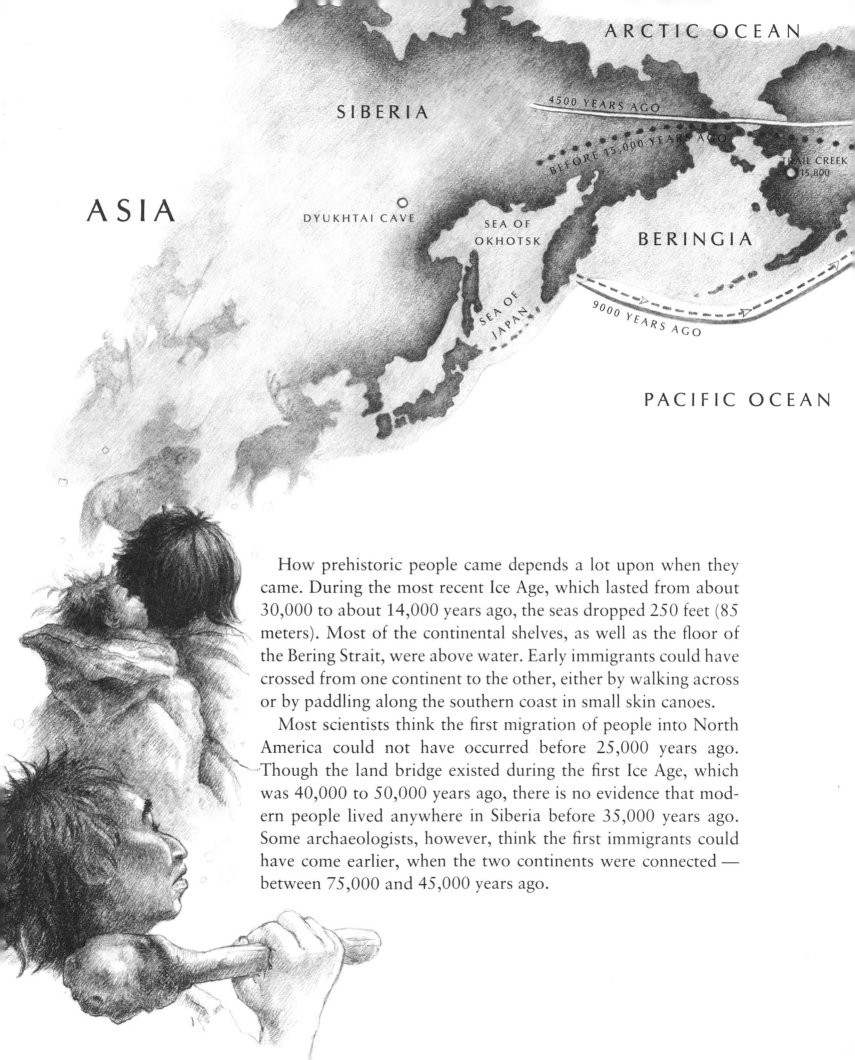

ARCTIC OCEAN

SIBERIA

4500 YEARS AGO

BEFORE 15,000 YEARS AGO

TRAIL CREEK
15,800

ASIA

DYUKHTAI CAVE

SEA OF
OKHOTSK

BERINGIA

SEA OF
JAPAN

9000 YEARS AGO

PACIFIC OCEAN

How prehistoric people came depends a lot upon when they came. During the most recent Ice Age, which lasted from about 30,000 to about 14,000 years ago, the seas dropped 250 feet (85 meters). Most of the continental shelves, as well as the floor of the Bering Strait, were above water. Early immigrants could have crossed from one continent to the other, either by walking across or by paddling along the southern coast in small skin canoes.

Most scientists think the first migration of people into North America could not have occurred before 25,000 years ago. Though the land bridge existed during the first Ice Age, which was 40,000 to 50,000 years ago, there is no evidence that modern people lived anywhere in Siberia before 35,000 years ago. Some archaeologists, however, think the first immigrants could have come earlier, when the two continents were connected — between 75,000 and 45,000 years ago.

OLD CROW
BASIN

BLUEFISH CAVE
15,000

NORTH
AMERICA

MARMES
ROCK-SHELTER
13,000

WILSON BUTTE, ID
15,000

SELBY, CO
20,000(?)

FORT ROCK
CAVE, OR
14,000

DUTTON, CO
20,000(?)

BURNHAM SITE,
OK   26,000(?)

CLOVIS, NM
11,500

MEADOWCROFT
ROCK-SHELTER,
PA 19,000

VALSEQUILLO,
MEXICO
22,000

TLAPACOYA,
MEXICO
22,000

TAIMA-TAIMA,
VENEZUELA
14,500

PIKIMACHAY CAVE,
PERU
25,000(?)

JAYAMACHAY,
PERU
22,000(?)

PEDRA FURADA,
BRAZIL
32,000(?)

SOUTH
AMERICA

MONTE VERDE, CHILE
34,000-14,000(?)

TIERRA DEL FUEGO,
CHILE (FELL'S CAVE)
11,000

Numbers on map indicate the number of years ago for which
dated evidence exists of human presence. Dates not universally
accepted as proven are marked (?).

MIGRATION ROUTES AND PRE-CLOVIS SITES

FIRST WAVE
ALEUTS
ATHABASKANS
POSSIBLE COASTAL ROUTE
EXPOSED CONTINENTAL SHELF

Although, as far as we know, modern humans were not in eastern Asia that early, there were Neanderthals living along the edge of ice sheets in eastern Russia as recently as 40,000 years ago. Neanderthals were a culturally advanced subgroup of *Homo sapiens*. They inhabited areas of Europe, northern Africa, and eastern Asia until they became extinct about 35,000 years ago, possibly because they intermixed with modern *Homo sapiens*. Neanderthals had shovel-shaped teeth like those of many Native Americans and Siberians, and they were well adapted to very cold climates. Even though no evidence has been found as yet that Neanderthals lived so far north as Beringia, this fact does not necessarily mean they did not.

Whenever the earliest settlers came, they must have been strong, hardy people, sophisticated in ways to survive harsh environments. They were undoubtedly hunters, fishers, and gatherers who already knew how to live in cold climates. They probably just wandered across Beringia in search of food. They may have been following the plentiful supply of game animals or looking for new supplies of wild plants to eat. Evidence shows that the earliest Americans ate a well-balanced diet of meat, seeds, berries, roots, insects, mollusks, fish, and anything else edible they could find. They probably didn't realize they were entering a continent where no humans had ventured before.

Beringia was a large, broad area. It was not much different from northeastern Asia where they had been living. Although no ice sheets or glaciers covered either, the climate was severe. Winters were nine degrees colder than they are in that area today.

They were also drier, with a thin snow cover and strong winds that whipped up huge sand dunes. Many of these sand dunes can still be found in western Alaska. The summers were short and may have been warmer and drier than they are today.

The first Americans protected their bodies and feet from severe cold by wearing furs and skins of animals they killed. Hides were sewn together with bone needles and animal sinew. The earliest settlers used fire to heat their homes and cook their food and perhaps to scare away predators. Fossils of bears, dire wolves, cheetahs, saber-toothed tigers as big as horses, and jaguars as big as lions have been found in Beringia.

These people probably lived in tents with frames of mammoth or mastodon bones, which they covered with furs held down at the bottom by stones. Remains of shelters such as these have been found in northern Asia where people were living about 40,000 years ago. Beringian mammoths, horses, and musk-oxen had thick woolly coats with long skirtlike fringes that hung down nearly to the ground, which would have made excellent robes and covers for tents. There was not enough snow cover on Beringia to build igloos, and large trees were rare, but dwarf birch and willow bushes probably grew on the floodplains and driftwood may have been plentiful.

Fossil pollen and fossil insects show that grasses, sedges, and wormwood grew in parts of Beringia. Perhaps the northern half was an Arctic tundra, but at least parts of the southern coast were treeless plains. There may have been many marshes and shallow ponds. There were certainly several large rivers. The willow shrubs and dwarf birch along the riverbanks were ideal food for large herbivores such as woolly mammoths, wild horses, steppe bison, caribou (reindeer), saiga antelope, musk-oxen, yaks, camels, mountain sheep, and beavers as big as bears that lived there. Swarms of flies and mosquitos probably plagued the earliest settlers in summer. Fossils of grassland beetles, ants, conifer-loving beetles, water insects, and dung beetles (which are always found where there are hoofed animals) also have been found in Beringia.

Predators and big game animals had been in Beringia since at least as early as 50,000 years ago. These animals probably came before humans, but where animals could go, humans could. Humans are capable of adapting to any environment. They have always sought to learn what is beyond the horizon. Throughout their history on earth, they have been on the move, covering enormous distances. Their movement into North America was just another step in their eastward migration.

Many archaeologists think that the earliest immigrants may have drifted into North America in a more or less continuous stream over several thousand years. Blood tests on modern Native Americans indicate that the first immigrants were the ancestors of all Native Americans south of Alaska except the Athabaskans (which includes the Apache, Navajo, and northwest coast tribes). The ancestors of the Athabaskans probably arrived around 14,000 years ago and the ancestors of the Eskimo-Aleuts (who live in Alaska and the northern coastal regions) probably immigrated to North America about 12,000 years ago. Studies based on blood tests indicate that both Athabaskans and Eskimo-Aleuts may have come from different parts of Asia than did the first migrants.

It is certain that by 13,000 years ago people had been on the continents long enough to have spread from Alaska to the southernmost tip of South America and from the Pacific Ocean to the Atlantic. The exact time of the first arrival, though, is the subject of much debate. Some archaeologists are convinced that the first settlers did not occupy Beringia much before 15,000 years ago, because there is no undisputed evidence of occupation before that time.

The majority of archaeologists, however, believe the first people probably came within the last 20,000 years. And a few think the first settlers could have arrived in the Americas as long as 100,000 years ago. Humans had spread to every other continent in the world by 50,000 years ago, and no major barriers blocked the crossing into America at that time. Other scientists think they have very good clues that suggest occupation of Beringia at least 30,000 years ago.

ASIA

NORTH AMERICA

CHAPTER TWO

Paleo-Indians in Beringia

THE PEOPLE LIVING in the Americas before 12,000 years ago are called Paleo-Indians. Almost everyone agrees that stone tools found at Bluefish Cave in the northern Yukon were used by Paleo-Indians 15,000 years ago. But scientists who think they have found evidence of occupation earlier than that haven't been able to prove it to everyone's satisfaction.

Discovery of human bones that could be dated accurately would be proof enough. Unfortunately, human bones that old are rarely found, because humans seem to have always favored living in caves and rock-shelters in wooded areas along streams or lakes. That is where most of the few early campsites discovered so far have been. The soil in wooded areas is very acid and bones rarely fossilize in acid soil. However, just because human bones haven't been found doesn't mean there aren't any to be found. Most sites are discovered by accident. There probably are many ancient human bones yet to be discovered.

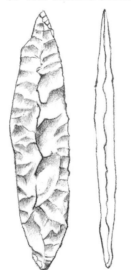

two views of a bifacially
flaked projectile head

Another way to prove that humans have occupied an area is to find their tools, but there aren't too many of these, either. The first Americans were nomadic hunters. People who move about a lot seldom burden themselves with unnecessary possessions or heavy materials. Stone tools, which are the most likely to have been preserved, would have been much too valuable to leave behind unless they were either broken or lost. Paleo-Indians were also ingenious and resourceful people who used whatever materials they found near at hand and what was most easily obtained. It is probable that they made tools from wood or bone because the right kind of rock for making them was often unavailable and would have been much too heavy to carry along. They already knew how to make tools by flaking bones the same way they did stone. Their ancestors had been flaking bones in Asia for a long time.

four views of a wedge-shaped
core, used to make tiny blades

Bone tools are lighter than stone tools, and every large animal that was killed furnished a new supply of fresh bone, which could be made into all the instruments needed for butchering animals and cleaning their hides. Unfortunately, unlike stone, wood and bone tools don't keep forever. Most of them decay into dust.

When scientists find artifacts (the discarded tools and other odds and ends of everyday life left behind by ancient peoples) they must prove that the objects were made by human hands. This is not always easy to do. Some of the tools made by early people, such as stone scrapers, look very much like stones that have been broken by natural forces. Similarly, bones broken by animals may be hard to tell from those broken by humans. However, expert archaeologists can usually tell them apart by studying them under an electron microscope.

microblade inserted into section of antler grooved by a burin makes a fine cutting edge
Onion Portage, AK

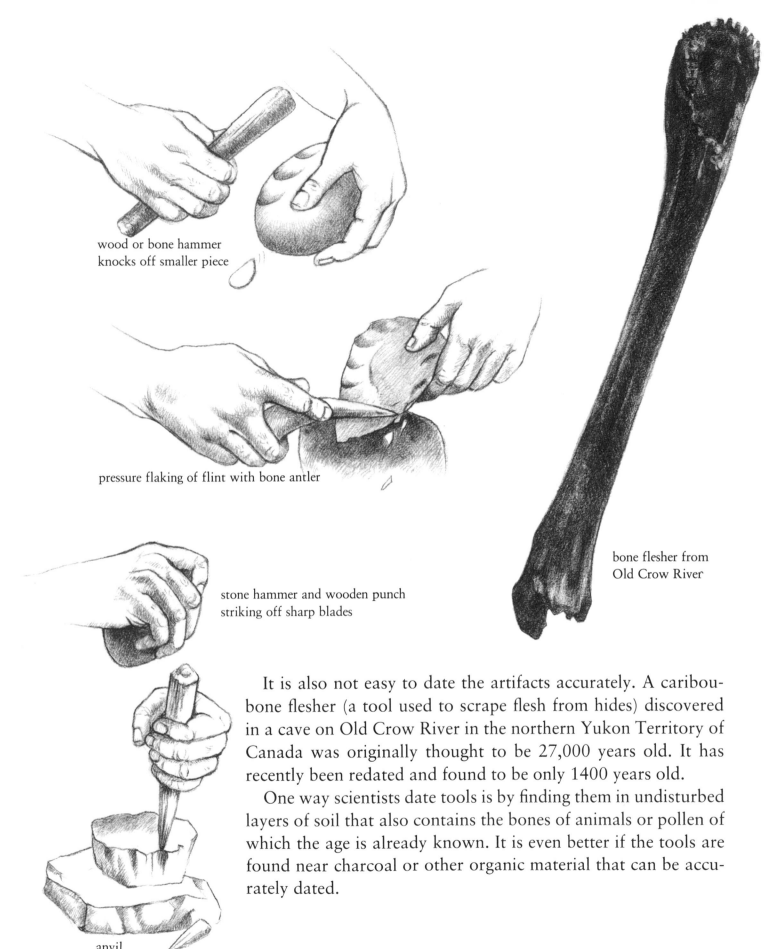

wood or bone hammer
knocks off smaller piece

pressure flaking of flint with bone antler

stone hammer and wooden punch
striking off sharp blades

bone flesher from
Old Crow River

anvil

It is also not easy to date the artifacts accurately. A caribou-bone flesher (a tool used to scrape flesh from hides) discovered in a cave on Old Crow River in the northern Yukon Territory of Canada was originally thought to be 27,000 years old. It has recently been redated and found to be only 1400 years old.

One way scientists date tools is by finding them in undisturbed layers of soil that also contains the bones of animals or pollen of which the age is already known. It is even better if the tools are found near charcoal or other organic material that can be accurately dated.

The approximate geological age of any organic material that is less than 50,000 years old can be determined by measuring the amount of carbon 14 it contains. All living things absorb a known amount of carbon 14 from the atmosphere. At death, the plant or animal no longer absorbs carbon 14, which begins to decay at a known rate. The amount that remains when the material is tested is the clue to the age of the sample. Unfortunately, it takes a lot of material to test in this manner. Sometimes whole bones are needed for the testing, and scientists are reluctant to use up entire artifacts in this way. However, a new and more accurate method of carbon dating using an accelerator requires much less material, and this method may soon be used to date all new discoveries. Other methods of dating have been used, but they are not considered very reliable by most archaeologists.

Canada's Old Crow River basin was once thought to provide evidence of the first immigrants in Beringia. Thousands of animal bones (mammoth, giant bison, and horses) were found with what were thought to be human-made stone and bone tools. The carbon 14 dates on the bones were 43,000 to 22,000 years ago. However, most archaeologists do not regard this as a valid site.

simulated diagram of a layer map to keep record of content of each layer

The date is considered unreliable because none of the material was found in undisturbed soil. The tools cannot be proven to be human-made because all of the material had been deposited at least once by running water. Natural forces could have fractured either the bone or the stone in the same way.

In an attempt to learn how to tell the difference between bone tools broken or flaked by humans and those broken by accident, a group of archaeologists experimented with the bones of a circus elephant that had just died of natural causes. They learned that most of the bones found at Old Crow River could have been broken by natural forces, but tools found at nearby Bluefish Cave could not have been made by accident. To make edged tools like those found in Bluefish Cave, the scientists had to strike a piece of bone in a special way and with a certain series of blows. The bone could be broken only while it was fresh; old bones will not flake. The scientists also learned that sharpened bone tools make excellent knives, and they were able to butcher the elephant with them.

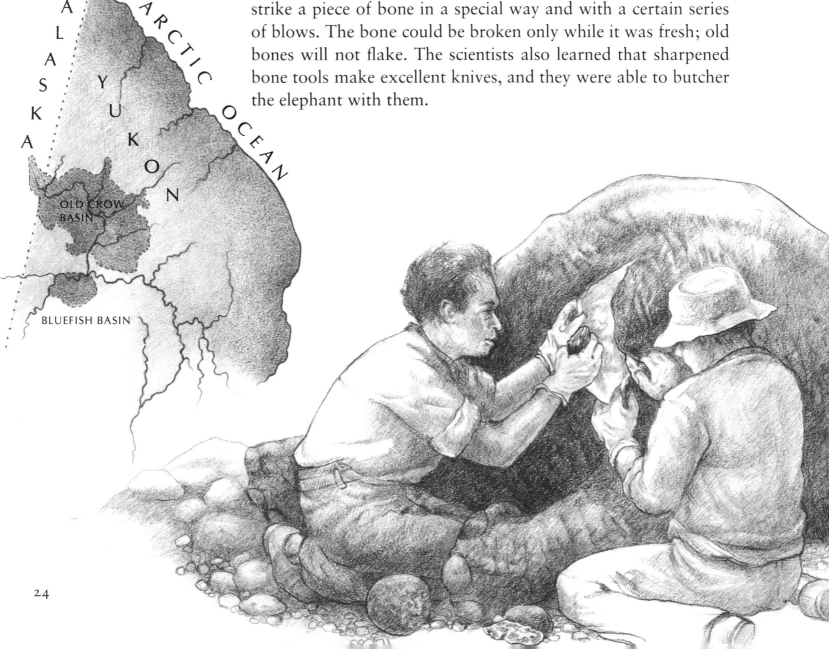

ARCTIC OCEAN

ALASKA

YUKON

OLD CROW BASIN

BLUEFISH BASIN

Bluefish Cave appears to have been an ancient butchering and toolmaking camp. A mammoth tooth, twice as large as a brick, was found in the cave along with fractured and flaked mammoth bones that had cutting edges suitable for butchering. There was also a leg bone of an extinct horse, which appears to have been broken for its marrow, but it can't be proven beyond all doubt that it was broken by humans.

The only dates for Bluefish Cave accepted by everyone are those of an upper level of occupation dated at 15,000 to 12,000 years ago. This level contained several stone tools along with animal bones that clearly show butchering marks when examined under a microscope. These Paleo-Indians made tools from rock they had brought to the caves from some distance. They left many stone trimming flakes, a chert graving tool, which they used for boring holes in stone, wood, or bone, and several microblades similar to those used in northeastern Siberia. Microblades are tiny blades made to fit in slots on a wooden or antler shaft. These blades are adequate proof that humans lived at Bluefish Cave 15,000 to 12,000 years ago. Thousands of tiny stone flakes and other artifacts found below that level are obviously older.

Small blade cores and bone projectile points with narrow, slotted grooves for holding microblade insets have been found in the lowest levels of two caves at Trail Creek, a tributary of Old Crow River in western Alaska. They were found with horse and bison bones dated 13,000 to 15,800 years old.

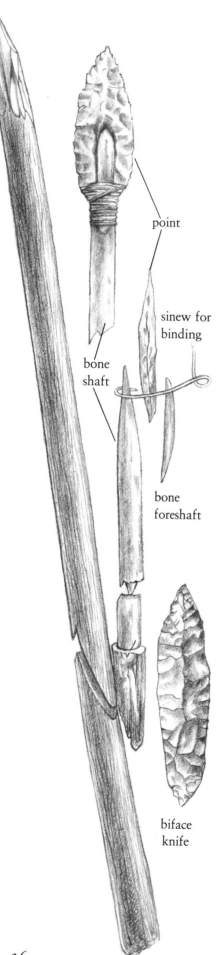

point

sinew for
binding

bone
shaft

bone
foreshaft

biface
knife

Although not everyone agrees, it is fairly well accepted that the Old Crow basin, as a whole, has been occupied since at least 15,000 years ago. Some claim the caves had been occupied 24,000 or even 40,000 years ago.

The Old Crow basin was an excellent place to live for humans already adapted to a cold climate. Many caves and rock-shelters along the bluffs bordering the valleys provided shelter from the strong winds. And from 80,000 to 22,000 years ago the basin teemed with game animals. Mammoth, bison, horse, two kinds of cameloid, moose, elk, fox, caribou, birds, and fish fed along or in the streams. The evidence seems to indicate that the earliest Americans in this area hunted with wooden spears, sharpened at the end or tipped with bone or stone blades. They may have been accompanied by dogs. Scientists have found fossilized jaws of several domesticated dogs that they believe to be at least 30,000 years old. If this date is accurate, these dogs were 20,000 years older than any other known domesticated dog and were undoubtedly the first dogs in America. There is no way of knowing whether the dogs were used by humans as pack animals or for hunting.

Some archaeologists think the reason more sites of very early Paleo-Indians haven't been found on Beringia is that many groups may have followed the southern coastline, which is now flooded by several hundred feet of ocean water. Others have suggested that the first settlers may have come before 40,000 years ago and the evidence of their presence may have been scoured away by later glaciers.

Whenever they came, it is certain that the resourceful first settlers of America continued to push onward. Evidence of their journeys to the south and east have been found in both North America and South America.

CHAPTER THREE

Beyond Beringia

ALTHOUGH ALMOST EVERYONE agrees that humans entered the Americas by way of Beringia, they don't all agree about the timing of their migration out of Beringia or the path of that migration. If they crossed earlier than most suppose, the period between 60,000 and 20,000 years ago seems to have been the best time to populate the new continents. Humans could have spread as far east as the Hudson Bay and as far south as they cared to go within that time. Large Asian mammals were already in the area of the United States by 40,000 years ago. There is no reason humans couldn't have gotten there too. They would have had to adapt to a variety of climates, but their ancestors had done that many times before.

Between 25,000 and 14,000 years ago, except for along the coast, conditions for migration out of Beringia became less favorable. But even then passage wasn't impossible. There was only a relatively short period when there was no open corridor between the glaciers.

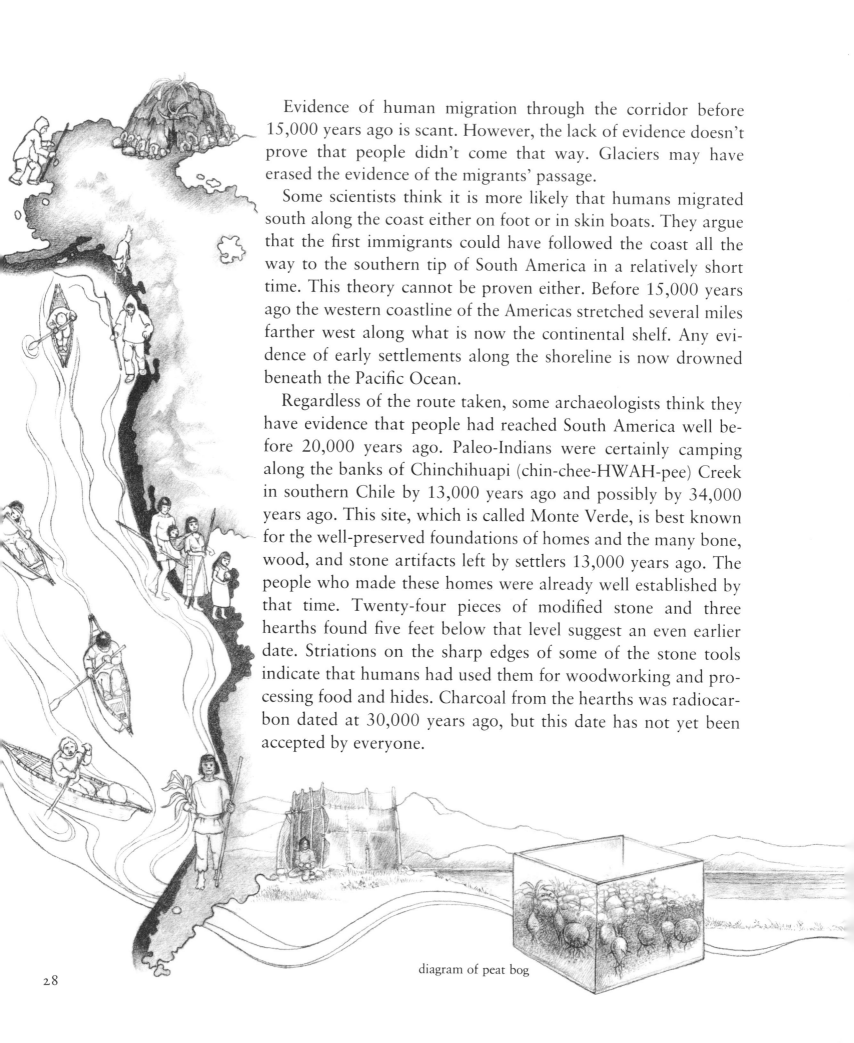

Evidence of human migration through the corridor before 15,000 years ago is scant. However, the lack of evidence doesn't prove that people didn't come that way. Glaciers may have erased the evidence of the migrants' passage.

Some scientists think it is more likely that humans migrated south along the coast either on foot or in skin boats. They argue that the first immigrants could have followed the coast all the way to the southern tip of South America in a relatively short time. This theory cannot be proven either. Before 15,000 years ago the western coastline of the Americas stretched several miles farther west along what is now the continental shelf. Any evidence of early settlements along the shoreline is now drowned beneath the Pacific Ocean.

Regardless of the route taken, some archaeologists think they have evidence that people had reached South America well before 20,000 years ago. Paleo-Indians were certainly camping along the banks of Chinchihuapi (chin-chee-HWAH-pee) Creek in southern Chile by 13,000 years ago and possibly by 34,000 years ago. This site, which is called Monte Verde, is best known for the well-preserved foundations of homes and the many bone, wood, and stone artifacts left by settlers 13,000 years ago. The people who made these homes were already well established by that time. Twenty-four pieces of modified stone and three hearths found five feet below that level suggest an even earlier date. Striations on the sharp edges of some of the stone tools indicate that humans had used them for woodworking and processing food and hides. Charcoal from the hearths was radiocarbon dated at 30,000 years ago, but this date has not yet been accepted by everyone.

diagram of peat bog

28

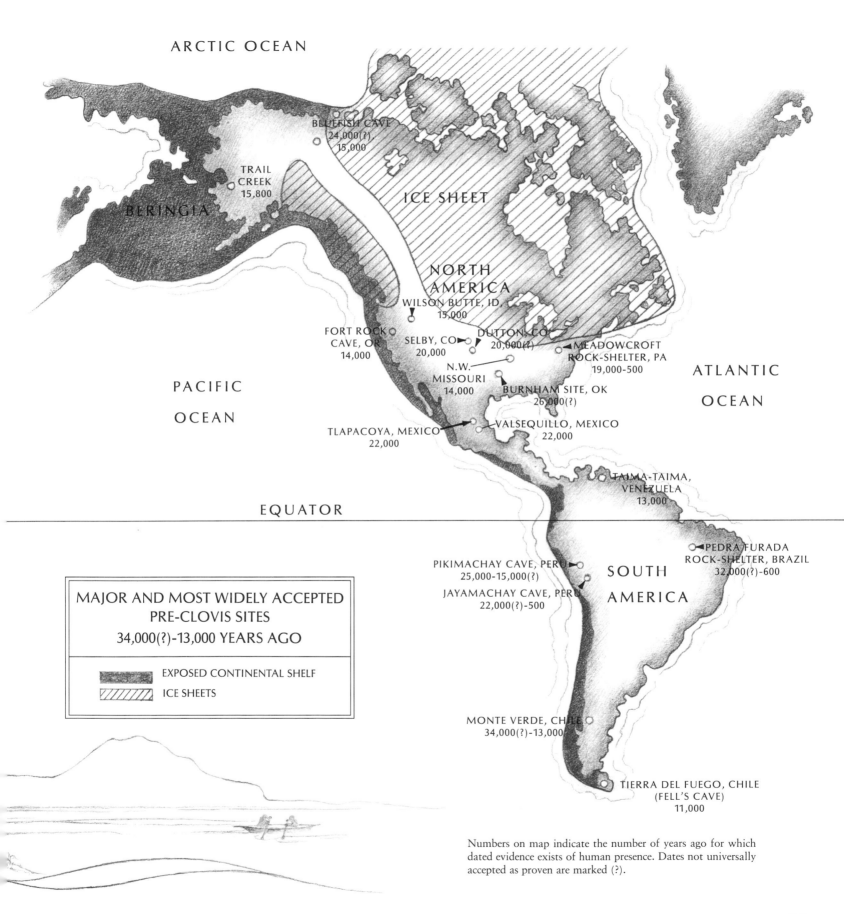

ARCTIC OCEAN

BLUEFISH CAVE
24,000(?)
15,000

TRAIL
CREEK
15,800

BERINGIA

ICE SHEET

NORTH
AMERICA

WILSON BUTTE, ID.
15,000

FORT ROCK
CAVE, OR
14,000

SELBY, CO
20,000

DUTTON, CO
20,000(?)

MEADOWCROFT
ROCK-SHELTER, PA
19,000-500

N.W.
MISSOURI
14,000

BURNHAM SITE, OK
26,000(?)

PACIFIC

OCEAN

TLAPACOYA, MEXICO
22,000

VALSEQUILLO, MEXICO
22,000

ATLANTIC

OCEAN

TAIMA-TAIMA,
VENEZUELA
13,000

EQUATOR

PEDRA FURADA
ROCK-SHELTER, BRAZIL
32,000(?)-600

PIKIMACHAY CAVE, PERU
25,000-15,000(?)

JAYAMACHAY CAVE, PERU
22,000(?)-500

SOUTH

AMERICA

MAJOR AND MOST WIDELY ACCEPTED
PRE-CLOVIS SITES
34,000(?)-13,000 YEARS AGO

EXPOSED CONTINENTAL SHELF

ICE SHEETS

MONTE VERDE, CHILE
34,000(?)-13,000

TIERRA DEL FUEGO, CHILE
(FELL'S CAVE)
11,000

Numbers on map indicate the number of years ago for which
dated evidence exists of human presence. Dates not universally
accepted as proven are marked (?).

29

early immigrants along coast of Beringia

By 13,000 years ago the Monte Verde people had become quite sophisticated and were far more advanced than anyone had ever suspected such early people could be. They lived in well-planned, permanent villages of thirty to fifty individuals and traded extensively with people as far away as the Pacific coast and the mountains of Argentina. More is known about the Monte Verde people than other Paleo-Indians because archaeologists found a large part of one of their villages buried in a bog. They discovered foundations of twelve houses, hundreds of wooden tools and other artifacts, sixteen medicinal plants, and forty-two edible plants. The plants had been stashed in storage pits. The log foundations and plants were well preserved because organic materials such as plant fiber and bone almost never decay when buried in bogs. Lack of oxygen in the bog and minerals in its water act as preservatives. The rectangular houses had walls made of branches covered with hide. These 13,000-year-old houses are the oldest known in the Americas. The Monte Verde people divided their villages into living and working areas. Much of their time must have been spent at woodworking because they left behind more wooden tools than stone.

a Monte Verde dwelling

Scientists who discovered the Pedra Furada rock-shelter in northeastern Brazil believe people lived there from about 32,000 to 6000 years ago. They say new evidence suggests some people may have lived there from 45,000 to 5000 years ago, but few other archaeologists are convinced the caves were occupied that early.

The rock-shelter, located on the side of a steep sandstone cliff above the Pedra Furada valley, appears to have been a temporary campsite where hunters manufactured stone tools and perhaps performed rituals. They built circular stone hearths near the back of the cave. Hunting bands apparently stopped there regularly to make tools and cook food, sometimes reusing old hearths. Several broken quartz and quartzite tools along with hundreds of stone flakes, apparently leftovers from manufacturing or resharpening tools, lay near the hearths. Scientists think the settlers manufactured tools in the cave and took them to permanent villages in the valley below because very few finished tools were found.

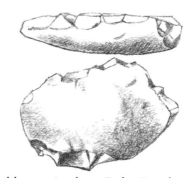

blunt point from Pedra Furada

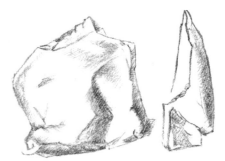

notched point made of quartz flake from Pedra Furada

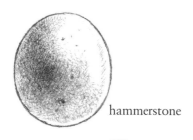

hammerstone

quartzite cobblestone

drawing on rock
at Pedra Furada

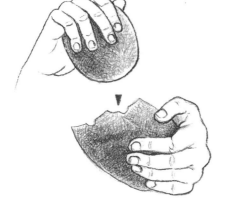

Pedra Furada people made chopping tools, burins (tools for carving wood or bone), notched pieces, and double-edged flaked tools. No wood or bone artifacts were found here, but the acid soil in this area would not preserve wood or bone.

As time passed the occupants of the cave began making better tools and living more sophisticated life-styles. Some time along the way, possibly as early as 17,000 years ago, they began decorating the walls and ceilings of the cave with red and yellow ochre. Paint chips on a stone believed to have fallen from the ceiling were radiocarbon dated at 17,000 years ago. This was about the same time people in Europe, Africa, and Australia were decorating their caves. By 12,000 years ago the Pedra Furada people had painted 240 rock-shelters in Brazil. The earliest cave artists of Europe painted only animals. The first American artists painted humans in everyday activities as well as animals. Some of their pictures showed people using spear-throwers similar to those used by Amazon Indians until quite recently. The Amazon spears had wooden projectile points.

early hand axe made by striking
a cobblestone with a hammerstone

Pikimachay (pee-kee-MAH-chai), or Flea Cave, which is located in the Andes Mountains of Peru, may have been occupied from 25,000 to 15,000 years ago. It would have held a lot of people. The mouth of the cave is six stories high and as wide as half a city block. The floor is eighty feet (the length of a passenger coach on a train) from front to back. Its earliest occupants made crude tools — sidescrapers, cleavers, sawtooth forms, and spokeshaves, tools used to plane wood. One of the tools was made from a green stone that had come from far away.

Hunting bands used the cave possibly between 20,000 and 14,000 years ago. These people made more sophisticated tools of flint, basalt, chalcedony, chert, and quartzite. They left hundreds of tools including leaf-shaped points, choppers, spokeshaves, scrapers, burins, gravers, sidescrapers, fluted-edged blades, bone awls and scrapers, and an antler punch. Bones of extinct horses, camels, deer, saber-toothed tigers, and an elephant-sized ground sloth lying alongside tools and many bone and stone flakes suggest to scientists that these people butchered animals and knapped (chipped off pieces) flint and bone tools in Flea Cave.

perforator point found
at Flea Cave

bone from sloth found at Flea Cave

ground sloth (*Megatherium*)

El Jobo point

Jayamachay (ha-yah-MAH-chai), or Pepper Cave, located in the same general area as Flea Cave, may have been occupied by bands of hunters from 22,000 years ago to 500 years ago. This cave was nearly as wide as Flea Cave but only fifteen feet deep. Human bones were found at the 14,000-year level.

Five hundred separate sites have been found in the forested valley below these two caves. Similar very early occupation sites were found in Ecuador, Colombia, and other South American countries. By 13,000 years ago Paleo-Indians may have been hunting mastodons throughout South America. Evidence of this was found at Taima-Taima, an ancient watering hole in northern Venezuela where an El Jobo point was found lying in the pelvis of a young mastodon. The kill was dated from twigs believed to have been the stomach contents of the mastodon.

Although the evidence of early arrival in South America is impressive, the dates are hotly debated. The evidence of early arrival in North America is much poorer. Some archaeologists use this to strengthen the argument for at least some coastal migration routes. There are, however, a few sites that suggest an inland route of migration in North America.

CHAPTER FOUR

Paleo-Indians in North America

22,000 TO 12,500 YEARS AGO

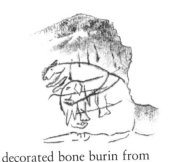

decorated bone burin from
Valley of Mexico

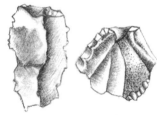

obsidian blade

andesite blades from Tlapacoya

IF HUMANS WERE in South America by 30,000 years ago they must have passed through North America much earlier than that unless they traveled along the coast. So far scientists have found very little evidence to prove that people were in North America before 20,000 years ago. Very old tools have been found lying on the surface in Mexico and Central America. Unfortunately, surface artifacts can't be dated.

However, bone and stone tools found in the Valley of Mexico suggest that the general area where Teotihuacán later developed was well populated as early as 22,000 years ago. The tools were found near hearths containing wood and charred animal bones at several different sites. The Paleo-Indians apparently butchered and cooked Ice Age animals at their campsites. Scientists found mammoth, horse, bison, cameloid, black bear, deer, and mastodon bones beside hearths near Valsequillo (VAL-see-KWIL-oh) and Tlapacoya (tlah-pah-KOH-yah). Food must have been plentiful in the valley, because these people had enough spare time to decorate some of the bones. They used a stone burin to scratch

hearth at Tlapacoya

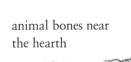

animal bones near
the hearth

obsidian blade left behind
by Paleo-Indians in Valley
of Mexico

pictures of game animals on mastodon bones. When these people moved on, they left behind stone choppers, points, sidescrapers, wedges, end scrapers, and spokeshaves.

Some scientists have suggested that people were in the Valley of Mexico as early as 35,000 years ago, but this date is not widely accepted. The carbon 14 test yielding this date was run on a snail shell found near tools. Dates from snail shells are not always accurate. However, an obsidian blade found buried beneath a tree trunk is thought to be at least 24,000 years old. The tree has been radiocarbon dated at 23,000 years ago and dates of fossil tree trunks usually are accurate. Since the blade was buried beneath the tree, it is probably older than 23,000 years.

Curiously, no well-documented sites before 20,000 years ago have been found in the area of the United States. Claims of 200,000 and 40,000 years ago have been made for sites in California, but the evidence is considered very poor by most archaeologists. Some question whether the tools found at these sites were man-made. Others consider the dating method used unreliable. A human skull found in Los Angeles has been dated at 23,600 years ago, but this date is also controversial.

A couple of recent discoveries, however, may prove to be more reliable in filling the gap. In 1991 a scientist looking for pollen and other evidence of early agriculture in a cave on a firing range at Fort Bliss, New Mexico, found something even more exciting. He discovered evidence that leads him to believe Paleo-Indians inhabited the region from 36,000 years ago to 10,000 years ago. The evidence includes a 24,000-year-old toe bone of a horse with an arrow point embedded in it, and a clay fireplace that appears to have a human thumbprint in it. The fireplace has been dated at 36,000 years ago. Although the evidence is convincing and the site appears to be fairly well documented, the site will have to be studied by many other archaeologists before the dates are proven accurate and it is accepted as valid.

Paleo-Indians may have arrived in northwestern Oklahoma by 26,000 years ago according to a single radiocarbon date. While digging a farm pond a farmer uncovered what appears to be an ancient butchering site near a watering hole. Although it will require much more study to be sure this date is accurate, at present it seems promising. The butchers left behind two broken flint tools, a smooth stone that someone must have carried to

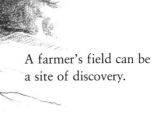

A farmer's field can be a site of discovery.

the site, part of a bear's paw that appears to have butchering marks on it, and fingernail-size flint flakes made when tools were sharpened. A prehistoric bison skull lay near the flakes. Bones of prehistoric horses and mammoth or mastodon were also found near the watering hole.

Farmers who were digging irrigation ditches and ponds near the towns of Selby and Dutton in Colorado uncovered several mammoth bones that have been tentatively dated at from 20,000 to 11,500 years ago. Some of the bones had been flaked and polished from use, suggesting that humans had camped there. Other bones left around the campsites indicated these Paleo-Indians hunted small mammals as well as mammoth, camel, horses, sloths, peccaries, and bison on the Colorado plains. The hunters killed large animals with spears tipped with long, slender bone or wooden points. Apparently they hacked off the animal's head, tail, and feet, then either pulled or carried the body back to the campsite to be butchered. The earliest inhabitants of these sites left behind only bone tools, which were not very different from the tools found at Old Crow basin in the Yukon.

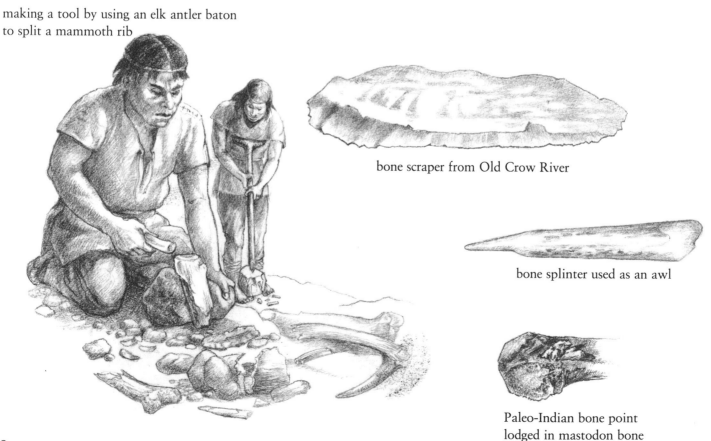

making a tool by using an elk antler baton to split a mammoth rib

bone scraper from Old Crow River

bone splinter used as an awl

Paleo-Indian bone point lodged in mastodon bone

40

The best evidence of early Paleo-Indians in eastern North America was found at Meadowcroft Rock-shelter located on the north bank of Cross Creek in southwestern Pennsylvania. This roomy, fifty-foot-long, twenty-foot-deep rock-shelter was an ideal place for early campers. It had a southern exposure and was well ventilated. People may have occupied it continuously from about 20,000 to 200 years ago.

The earliest inhabitants left behind stone tools and a small piece of a mat or basket woven from strips of bark. The bark has been carbon 14 dated at 19,600 years ago. But again not all archaeologists accept this early date because at that time the ice sheet was only thirty-six miles north of Meadowcroft. The earliest Meadowcroft people may have woven mats for sleeping on or baskets for gathering wild plant food. Perhaps they made both. Archaeologists know they gathered wild plants for food. They found the evidence in storage pits dug in the floor of the rock-shelter.

It is believed that small bands of people may have met at Meadowcroft. During the time they were there they cooked rabbit and deer over roasting pits. While their dinner cooked, they

blade from Meadowcroft

biface blade from Meadowcroft

Mungai knife

Miller lanceolate point

sat around the campfire and sharpened stone and bone tools for the next hunt. One of the tools they left behind was a small, tapered, willow leaf–shaped projectile point. Scientists named this point the Miller lanceolate point after the owner of the Meadowcroft property. They think the presence of this point suggests that the people who used the rock-shelter also hunted big game. They left behind unifaced knives, too. These knives are flaked on only one side. Scientists call them Mungai knives in honor of a helpful local farmer and amateur archaeologist. Other tools found at Meadowcroft are bifacial cutting and slicing tools, gravers (thought to be used in working bone or wood), and several small three-sided blades twice as long as they are wide. The only bone tool found at this level was a piece of deer antler, which was possibly used as a hammer to remove small flakes from stone tools.

Paleo-Indians occupied Meadowcroft more or less continuously from 19,000 to 12,000 years ago. Several sites indicate that Paleo-Indians were spread widely across the United States by 13,000 years ago. They occupied Wilson Butte Cave in central Idaho between 15,000 and 13,000 years ago. They also were living in Fort Rock Cave in Oregon and in northwestern Missouri by 14,000 years ago. These people were skilled stoneworkers. They made bifacial projectile points and may have been ancestors of the Clovis people.

CHAPTER FIVE

The Big Game Hunters

12,000 TO 7000 YEARS AGO

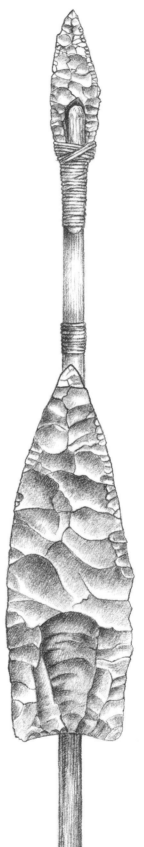

THE CLOVIS PEOPLE were very successful big game hunters who first appeared in the western plains soon after the glaciers began to retreat. Some scientists think the Clovis people were the first American settlers and that they arrived sometime after 15,000 years ago. Others think they were descendants of immigrants who arrived much earlier. Scientists may disagree about who the Clovis people were, but everyone agrees that they were thriving over wide areas of North and South America by 11,500 years ago. Within just a few centuries they had spread from coast to coast. Thousands of their artifacts have been found linking river valley to river valley from Washington State to Nova Scotia and from Alaska to the southern tip of South America. Scientists identify Clovis people by the distinctive fluted (grooved) spear points they made. These points are called Clovis points because they were first found near Clovis, New Mexico. Clovis points have since been found all over North America and in many places in Central and South America.

Clovis points were made with shallow flutes or grooves on both sides at the base so that they could fit snugly around the shaft.

ARCTIC OCEAN

ICE
SHEET

NORTH
AMERICA

MARMES
ROCK-SHELTER

RICHEY-ROBERTS
WASHINGTON CLOVIS CACHE

HELL GAP, WY

NOVA SCOTIA

ATLANTIC
OCEAN

SHRIVE SITE, MO

CALIFORNIA

CLOVIS, NM

RUSSELL CAVE, AL

PACIFIC OCEAN

LITTLE SALT SPRING, FL

FOLSOM, NM

EQUATOR

SOUTH
AMERICA

CLOVIS AND FOLSOM SITES

12,000-8000 YEARS AGO

FELL'S CAVE
TIERRA DEL FUEGO,
CHILE

There is little doubt that Clovis points were used to kill mammoths and mastodons. Some of the points were found embedded in the bones of these animals. Some of the animals were killed with hand-held spears, others were killed with spears thrown by a spear-thrower (atlatl). Spears thrown with an atlatl can go farther and faster than hand-thrown spears.

The Clovis people chose the finest-grained stone — obsidian, flint, chert, jasper, quartz, or chalcedony — to make their points. Some of this stone came from nearby, but some came from as far as 186 miles away from the Clovis site. The hunters either traveled great distances to get the stone or traded with other bands for it. Clovis points were beautifully made and must have been highly valued. They were seldom left behind, because it required a lot of work and a great deal of skill to make a Clovis point. First the hunter trimmed a flake by carefully striking it with a hammerstone on both sides to give it the right shape. Then he grooved it with a bone punch. Since this was time-consuming work, the tips were resharpened when they were damaged, causing the points to change shape with use. The trimming flakes were often used to make other tools.

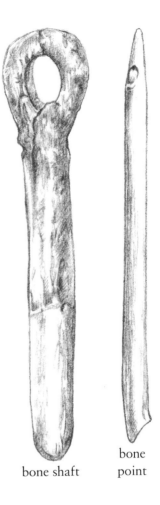

bone shaft

bone point

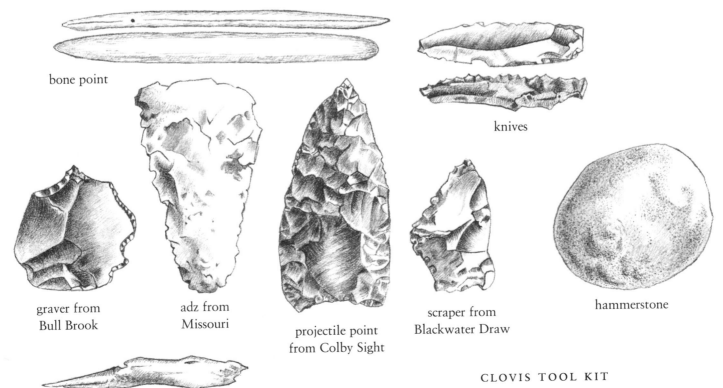

bone point

knives

graver from Bull Brook

adz from Missouri

projectile point from Colby Sight

scraper from Blackwater Draw

hammerstone

CLOVIS TOOL KIT

bone awl from Russell Cave

45

The largest and most beautiful Clovis points ever found are a matched pair made of clear chalcedony. These nearly nine-inch-long (twenty-two centimeters) points were found in an apple orchard in north central Washington State where they had been buried with seventeen other tools 12,000 years ago. Most Clovis points were less than half that size. The Washington points were very sharp and may have been used to butcher as well as kill animals. Traces of bison blood found on one of them suggest that it had been used as a butchering tool.

atlatl   spear

Clovis people were nomadic. They lived in small bands, moving often as they followed the herds. Some may have sought protection from cold winter storms in nearby caves or rockshelters, but they usually camped along the edge of streams and rivers where they ambushed game animals that came to drink. Thousands of sharpening flakes left among piles of bones near ancient watering holes suggest that the animals were butchered where they fell. The meat and hides were probably carried back to camp.

food storage pit

People living in Fell's Cave at the tip of South America used Clovis points to hunt guanaco, llama, and horses. But in North America the animals most often hunted with Clovis points were mammoth, mastodon, giant bison, and caribou. However, horse, camel, tapir, bear, and rabbit were also eaten. Large animals were important to the economy of these people. A single mastodon or mammoth provided enough meat to feed an entire band for months. Some of the meat was undoubtedly dried. Some northern hunters stored fresh meat in deep pits in the ground. Food storage pits, nearly twice the size of a refrigerator, were found in Nova Scotia, Michigan, and Maine. The hunters made weapons, shelters, and clothing from the hides, tusks, and bones. Fat was used in cooking or burned in bone lamps.

FROM FELL'S CAVE

fishtail
point

stemmed
point

Paleo-Indians used Clovis points for about 500 years, or until

the Ice Age big game animals died out. It is not known for sure why the big mammals became extinct. Of the more than seventy species of large mammals that once lived, only fifteen survived. The horse was not one of them. The hunting practices of the Clovis people have been blamed for the extinction of the large mammals, and they may have contributed to their extinction, but the change in climate probably had more to do with it. The climate was much drier after the glaciers retreated and, as a result, there was less grass for large mammals to eat. The large foraging animals such as mammoths, mastodons, horses, camels, and giant bison, as well as the large predators, such as the saber-toothed tiger, that preyed on them, required huge amounts of food. When the grass became too sparse, these animals became extinct. Only smaller species that required less food survived.

Early Americans adapted well to the change. Many switched to hunting caribou and a smaller species of bison. A somewhat different set of tools was used to hunt the smaller animals. The spearpoints were smaller and better made than Clovis points. These are called Folsom points, because they were first found near Folsom, New Mexico. With them were other tools and the bones of twenty-three bison. One of the points was found between the ribs of a bison. At a site in Missouri, a Folsom point was found embedded in a bison's spinal cord.

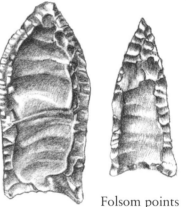

Folsom points

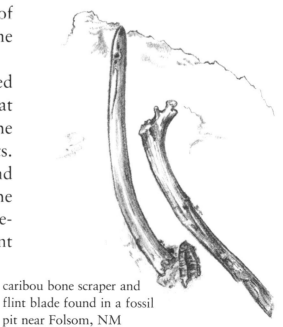

caribou bone scraper and flint blade found in a fossil pit near Folsom, NM

The Folsom point was one of the finest flint points made by early people anywhere in the world. Its shape was different from that of any other point. The base of the point was fishtailed and the point was fluted from base to tip. Its edges were sharpened by applying pressure with an antler wand (shaping rod) instead of being struck with a hammerstone.

Folsom points have been found in widely scattered areas of North and South America and in Mexico and Guatemala. Folsom people were camping regularly in Russell Cave in Alabama 9000 years ago. It is thought that they probably roamed the area outside the cave as early as 10,000 years ago. Native Americans continued to use the cave for shelter until well after the European settlers arrived. The cave could accommodate a fairly large

group. Its mouth is two stories high and wider than a basketball court is long. Many of the tools left in the cave by the earliest Folsom settlers closely resemble tools used in the far north. Some scientists think this may have been an area where migrants from the north met migrants from the west. Besides Folsom points, scientists found knife handles made of grooved bear teeth and a type of fishhook common among Arctic people but unknown this far south. Scientists also found a torch made from a hollowed leg bone of a bear. Filled with bear fat and given a fiber wick, the torch provided as much light as a candle.

a fine Folsom point flaked with a bone point

Not all of the people living in North America during this period were nomadic big game hunters. Some bands seem to have settled down permanently in areas where there was plenty of food or other needed resources. A band occupied the Palouse River Canyon in the state of Washington for about 11,000 years. A rock-shelter in one of the canyon walls may have been used for ritual ceremonies and burials. Inside the rock-shelter scientists found what they think was a cremation hearth and, buried in shallow graves, the remains of three humans, one of whom was a young child. Scientists call these people Marmes after the owner of the land. Outside the rock-shelter a cemetery where more than twenty-three people had been buried was discovered. This cemetery seems to have been used from 11,000 to 200 years ago — longer than any other known cemetery in North America. The remains of these ancestors of today's Palouse Indians are the oldest human remains found in North America that have been accurately dated.

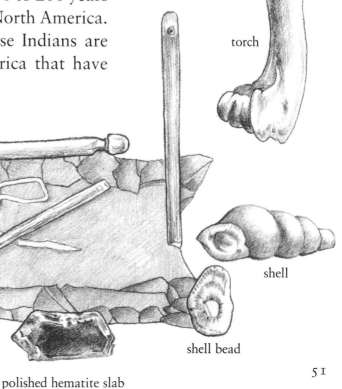

torch

shell

shell bead

ARTIFACTS FOUND
IN RUSSELL CAVE

bone fishhook   polished hematite slab

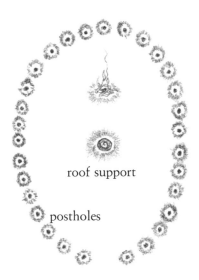

PLAN OF EARLY HOUSE
IN WYOMING

roof support

postholes

Another group of early Americans settled along the shores of an ancient lake in northern California near a large obsidian deposit. This area was apparently occupied from about 12,000 to 3000 years ago.

Evidence of the earliest known permanent house in North America was found in the Sierra Nevada Mountains east of San Francisco, California. This twelve-foot-long (3.5 meters), oval-shaped house had been built 10,000 years ago. It was dated from charcoal found in its hearth. The roof was probably supported by a pole set in the center of the packed clay floor. Remains of another house built 8000 years ago were found in Hell Gap, Wyoming. People lived in that area from 11,000 to 7000 years ago.

The region now occupied by Disney World and Kennedy Space Center in southern Florida was once the home of a large band of hunter-gatherers. The Florida People hunted game and gathered plant food in the region from 12,000 to 8000 years ago. Some camped for short periods around Little Salt Spring and other sinkholes. Experts think sinkholes were major water sources during that period, attracting wild animals and humans. At that time sea levels were low, and fossil pollens indicate that the climate of Florida was drier and cooler than it is today.

Human remains, artifacts, and bones of extinct animals found in and around Little Salt Spring reveal a great deal about the life of these people. Wooden stakes were set in the ground around the edge of the sinkhole, leaving only one way to get to the water. These may have been used to trap large animals that came to the sinkhole to drink. Bones of a ground sloth, young mammoth, rattlesnake, wood ibis, and bison were found in the cavern below the sinkhole.

today's water level

ledge

water level 12,000 years ago

ledge

The bones of a human and a giant land turtle's shell were found on a ledge several feet below the brim of the sinkhole. The man may have fallen into the sinkhole and not been able to get out. He managed to crawl onto the ledge, however, where he found the turtle. He apparently killed the turtle, turned it over, and cooked it in its own shell before he died 12,000 years ago.

People living in the area 9000 years ago left behind part of a carved oak mortar, which was probably used to grind seeds, and a nonreturning boomerang, which may be the oldest specimen of this type in the world.

By 8000 years ago the culture of the early Americans was becoming more and more sophisticated. The more skillful people became at hunting, fishing, and gathering, the more spare time they had to devote to other activities such as crafts and rituals. Someone carefully buried a little dog about the size of a fox terrier in a rock-shelter in Benton County, Missouri, about 7500 years ago. Dog burials became common practice among some later Native Americans, but this is one of the earliest we know about.

After 7000 years ago the culture of early Americans changed a great deal. People began making pottery, weaving cloth, and cultivating some of their food. Many lived in large towns. By and large their life-style was very much like that of any other people living at that time.

CHAPTER SIX

The Beginnings of Civilization

8000 TO 2000 YEARS AGO

As the climate cooled and water levels dropped, people living in central Florida began staying in one place for longer periods of time. Evidence of this was found in a peat bog near Kennedy Space Center when bulldozers were excavating for a housing development. The peat bog had been used as a burial ground more than 7000 years ago. One hundred seventy skeletons dating from 7000 to 8000 years ago were uncovered. The bones and artifacts buried with them reveal a great deal of exciting new information about the culture of the people who lived there. No other North American site has given us so much information. The burial customs of these early Floridians suggest a culture far more advanced than any other we know about for that period. The bodies had been wrapped in grass mats and covered with peat and wood before being placed in the bog. Remnants of clothing — finely woven cloth made from palm

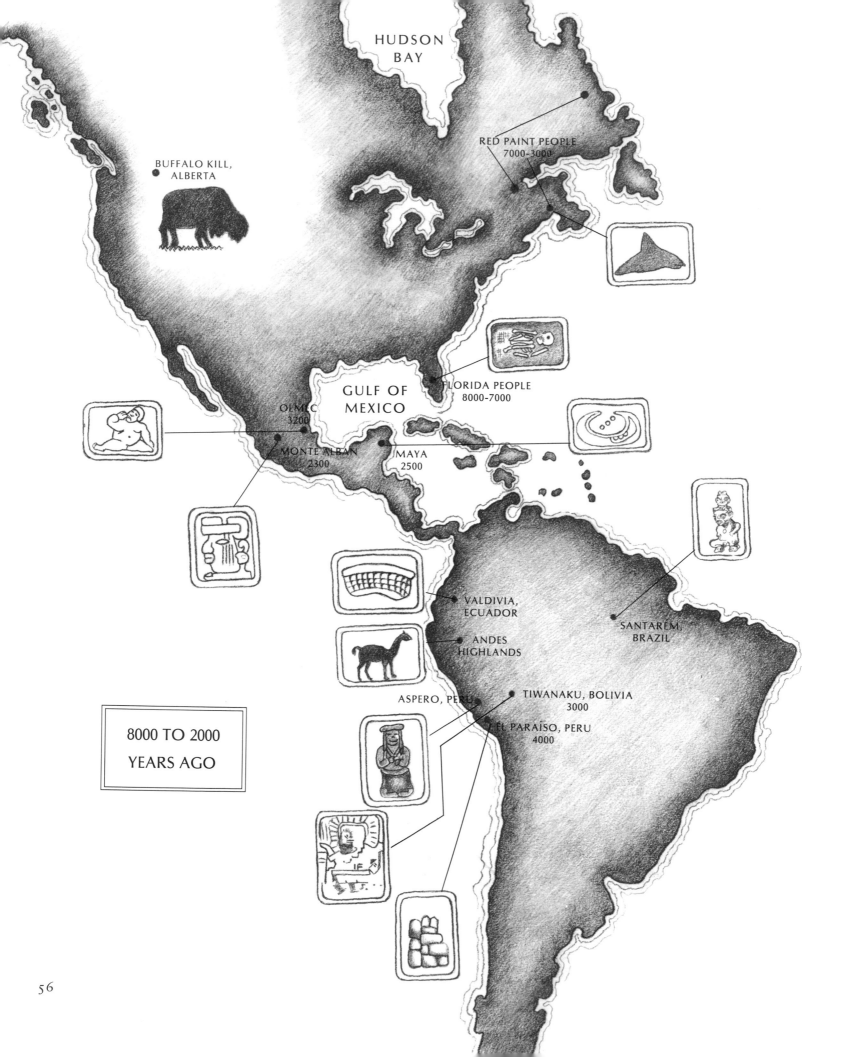

HUDSON
BAY

BUFFALO KILL,
ALBERTA

RED PAINT PEOPLE
7000-3000

GULF OF
MEXICO

FLORIDA PEOPLE
8000-7000

OLMEC
3200

MONTE ALBAN
2300

MAYA
2500

8000 TO 2000
YEARS AGO

VALDIVIA,
ECUADOR

SANTARÉM,
BRAZIL

ANDES
HIGHLANDS

ASPERO, PERU

TIWANAKU, BOLIVIA
3000

EL PARAÍSO, PERU
4000

fronds — still clung to some of the bodies. The mineral-rich water, depleted of oxygen, preserved the fabric, wood, mats, and bones. In fact, the skeletons were so well preserved that two of the skulls, one of a forty-five-year-old woman and one of a twenty-seven-year-old man, still contained brains. They are the oldest brains ever found.

Tools and ornaments were buried with many of the bodies. The most beautiful artifacts were in the graves of children and teen-agers. One teen-ager had been born with a crippling spinal disorder but apparently had been well cared for until his or her death. These pieces of evidence show that these early Floridians cherished their children and were caring people who were willing to support nonproductive persons for a long time.

Climatic changes forced hunting and gathering groups in many other areas, too, to find new methods of making a living. A variety of cultures developed as each group found different ways to use the natural resources in the regions where they lived.

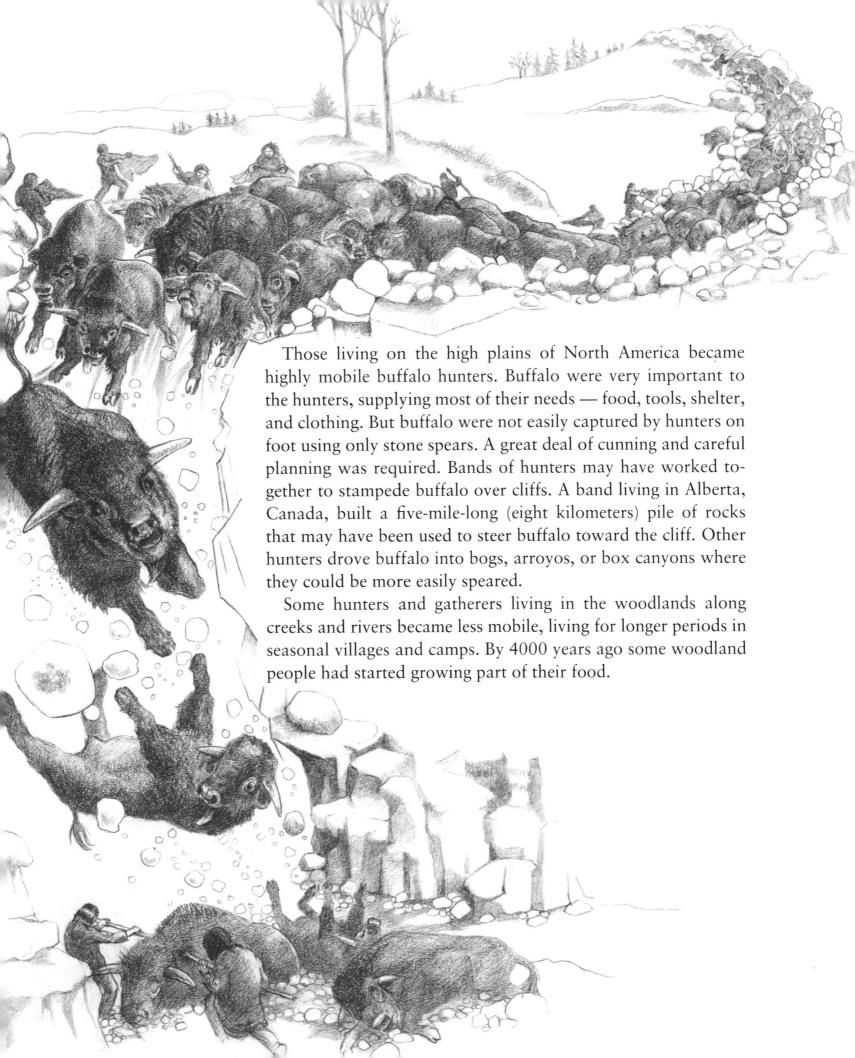

Those living on the high plains of North America became highly mobile buffalo hunters. Buffalo were very important to the hunters, supplying most of their needs — food, tools, shelter, and clothing. But buffalo were not easily captured by hunters on foot using only stone spears. A great deal of cunning and careful planning was required. Bands of hunters may have worked together to stampede buffalo over cliffs. A band living in Alberta, Canada, built a five-mile-long (eight kilometers) pile of rocks that may have been used to steer buffalo toward the cliff. Other hunters drove buffalo into bogs, arroyos, or box canyons where they could be more easily speared.

Some hunters and gatherers living in the woodlands along creeks and rivers became less mobile, living for longer periods in seasonal villages and camps. By 4000 years ago some woodland people had started growing part of their food.

sculpture of a whale
found in burial mound

cutaway view of burial mound in Labrador
showing well-preserved skeleton

People living along the northeastern seacoast hunted caribou in winter and harpooned sea mammals such as walrus and seals in summer. Archaeologists call these people the Red Paint People because pieces of red ochre were found in each of three stone-lined graves discovered in Quebec and Labrador. The graves were covered with mounds — five-foot-high piles of rock made of large boulders. These 7000-year-old mounds are the earliest known burial mounds found anywhere in the world. They were built to protect the graves, which were shallow because they were dug in rocky, subarctic terrain without the use of metal tools. Stone knives and projectile points were found in each grave. One grave contained a wooden spear, a harpoon-line holder, and one of the oldest toggling harpoons known. The grave of a young teen-ager contained a whistle made from the leg bone of a bird. Although broken, it still produces a shrill sound.

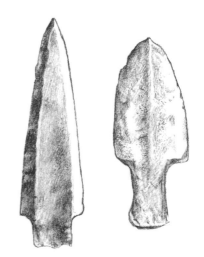

ground slate projectiles

ARTIFACTS FROM LABRADOR GRAVES

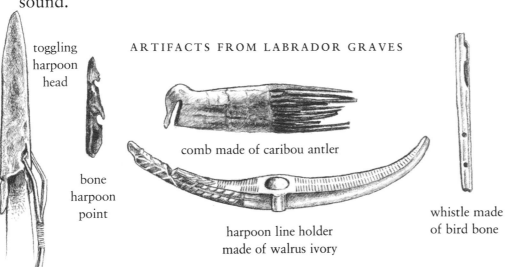

toggling
harpoon
head

bone
harpoon
point

comb made of caribou antler

harpoon line holder
made of walrus ivory

whistle made
of bird bone

making a dugout canoe

This culture was probably widespread along the Atlantic coast. Examination of 5000-year-old middens (garbage dumps) found in Maine show that these mound people ate caribou in winter but caught swordfish, blackfish, and porpoise in summer. Swordfish live only in the open sea and require a great deal of skill and large boats to catch. Stone axes and adz bits unearthed at the campsites lead scientists to believe these people made dugout canoes for sea fishing.

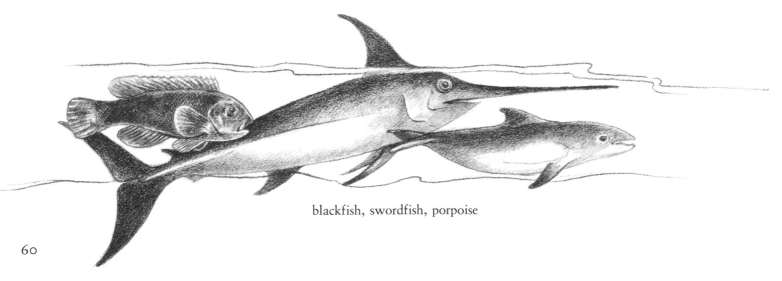

blackfish, swordfish, porpoise

Some of the nomadic hunters in the broad desert area that extended from Washington and Oregon to the Valley of Mexico became sedentary farmers who lived in permanent villages. Though the area was dry, it was rich in plant and animal life and, for a time, the people could live on what nature provided. As the population expanded, their needs became greater and they, too, began growing some of their food. Apparently the largest of the wild seeds were selected for sowing in garden patches near their villages. The populations grew even larger, and it became necessary to grow even more food, especially maize, which could be stored for the future. With plenty of food to eat, they had more time to paint pictures on canyon walls or make figurines of stone and willow and to devote to religious ceremonies.

Although the culture of early people in North America was becoming more and more highly developed, the earliest sites of advanced civilization have been found in South America. Evidence of some of the first domestication of plants in the New World was found in Peru. People living in the Andes highlands were growing peppers and gourds by 8500 years ago. Runner beans were a domesticated crop 7500 years ago. Seeds of these plants must have been imported from someplace else because they didn't grow naturally in this area, which clearly suggests a culture that had added farming to its ways of providing food for its people.

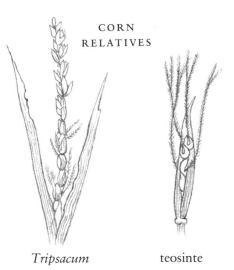

CORN RELATIVES

Tripsacum   teosinte

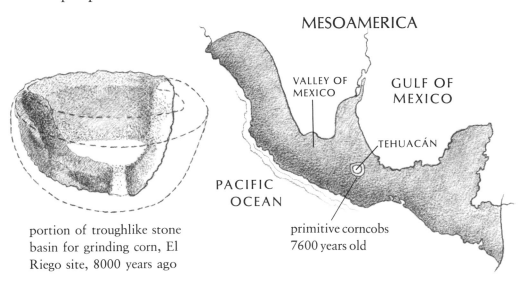

MESOAMERICA

VALLEY OF MEXICO

GULF OF MEXICO

TEHUACÁN

PACIFIC OCEAN

portion of troughlike stone basin for grinding corn, El Riego site, 8000 years ago

primitive corncobs 7600 years old

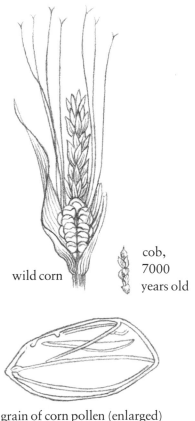

wild corn

cob, 7000 years old

grain of corn pollen (enlarged) that may be 80,000 years old, found in Mexico City lake bottom

61

foot plow

hoe

By 7000 years ago the people of the Andes highlands were living in closely grouped houses with clay floors, though they may have occupied them in summer only, because winters at such high altitudes can be very cold. By 5500 years ago they had domesticated llamas. At first, llamas were probably used more for food than as pack animals. The potato plant had been successfully domesticated by 5000 years ago.

The Andes highlands people apparently traded with people living in a narrow strip along the Pacific coast of southern Peru and northern Chile. There is evidence that they swapped obsidian for shellfish. Seashells have been found in Andean garbage dumps and Andean obsidian in seashore middens.

The coastal people had an entirely different life-style from those living in the Andes. This strip of land is one of the driest on earth, but the people lived well. Five thousand years ago their food came mostly from the Pacific Ocean, one of the richest sources of food on earth.

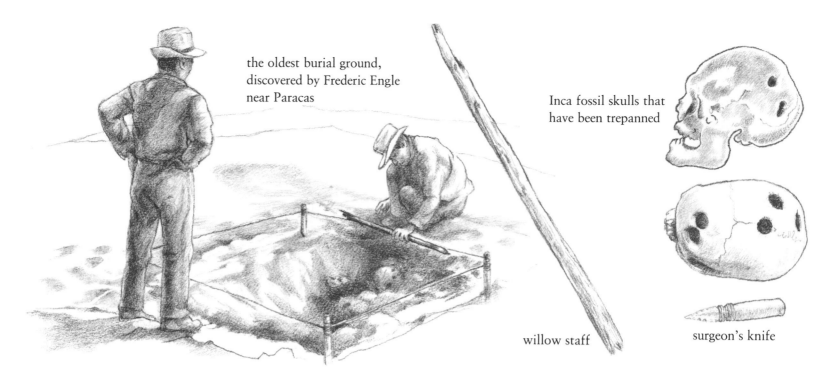

the oldest burial ground, discovered by Frederic Engle near Paracas

Inca fossil skulls that have been trepanned

willow staff

surgeon's knife

Twenty-five hundred almost-perfect mummified bodies of early coastal people have been found. They had been wrapped in reeds and leaves or cotton and placed in shallow graves, where they were preserved by dehydration. Most of the mummified bodies were less than 5000 years old, but some were 8000 years old — much older than Egyptian mummies. Scientific study of the mummies has told us a great deal about how these people lived.

These prehistoric people were about the same size as people living in the area today and their life spans were about as long. Many of them died of pneumonia. After 4000 years ago tuberculosis was also a common cause of death. They had fewer toothaches than people today, probably because they ate very few carbohydrates. Apparently their physicians were skilled surgeons, for some of the people had recovered from successful skull surgery. Using only volcanic glass tools and medicines they made themselves from native plants, these very early surgeons bored holes in the skulls of their patients to treat battle wounds and headaches. The evidence collected from the mummies shows that about half of the patients recovered because their wounds had healed. European doctors in the eighteenth century, using this same method with steel knives, had to abandon the practice because almost all their patients died.

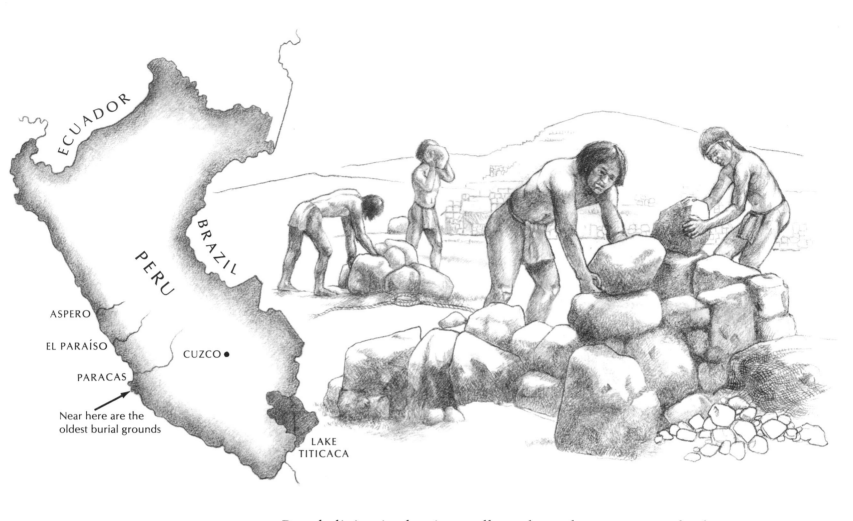

ECUADOR

BRAZIL

PERU

ASPERO

EL PARAÍSO

CUZCO •

PARACAS

Near here are the
oldest burial grounds

LAKE
TITICACA

ruin of section of platform

People living in the river valleys along these same sandy shores developed the first large cities in the Americas. These coastal people built the oldest known pyramids and monuments in the world. Several huge, U-shaped platform mounds and many smaller ones have been discovered at Aspero (ah-SPARE-o) and El Paraíso (pah-RYE-so). These 4000- and 5000-year-old centers were not actually cities but were ceremonial centers. Only priests and ruling classes lived there. Most of the people lived in villages surrounding these centers.

The monuments were apparently public structures, possibly religious temples, and were the center of community life. The tremendous work force needed to build them may have been organized by religious leaders from residents of the nearby villages.

These people still depended on the sea and wild plants, such as cattail rhizomes, for most of their food. But they also raised a fair share of their food in garden plots using simple sticks for digging tools. They cultivated gourds and cotton. The gourds were edible when young and also made excellent water containers when mature. Cotton, which didn't grow naturally in the area, was used to make fishnets and bags to hold rubble.

The pyramids were built of rubble, hauled to the site in bags by human laborers, and faced with blocks of basalt. The basalt blocks were quarried more than a half mile away. One pyramid required 100,000 tons of quarried stone to cover it.

Although the coastal people had no wheels, pottery, metal, or pack animals to help with the work, in many ways their accomplishments were more advanced than some of the Old World societies of the same period. The engineering skills of the coastal people were remarkable.

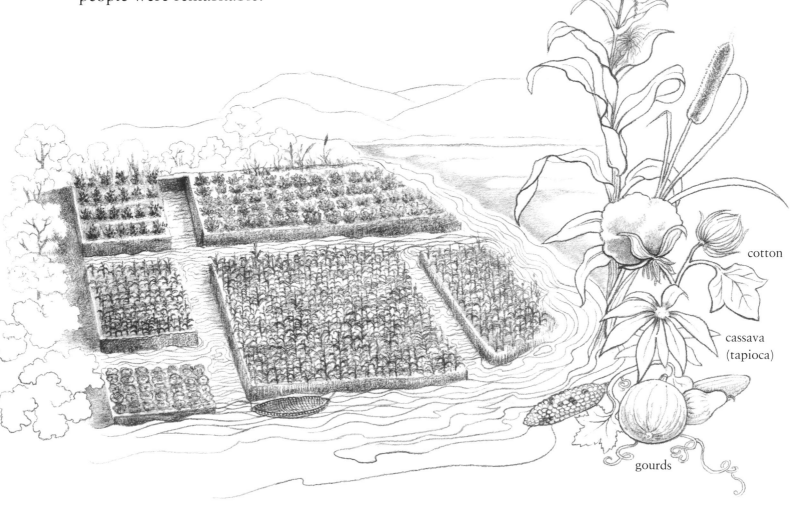

corn

cotton

cassava
(tapioca)

gourds

By 3700 years ago, about the time Hammurabi ruled Babylonia, the Peruvian coastal culture had developed a complicated agricultural technology along the river valleys. Extensive canals brought water great distances across the desert to irrigate large maize and yucca fields and to provide drinking water for their growing population. A powerful political system evolved to manage the large labor force needed to maintain the irrigation system and build bigger and better monuments. Some people spent their time weaving cloth and making pottery.

Not all advanced civilizations were in the valleys. Tiwanaku (tee-wahn-AHK-oo), Bolivia, a city of 40,000 people, was built 3000 years ago at an altitude of 12,630 feet (3850 meters). It is the highest known urban settlement of ancient America. By 2800 years ago the Chavin culture — forerunner to the Inca, the greatest of the Andean cultures — had already developed. Its huge temple complex contained some of the finest examples of Andean sculpture anyone has ever seen.

Another early cultural center was recently discovered in Brazil. Santarém, on the Tapajos (ta-pa-ZHOS) River, has been accelerator-radiocarbon dated at over 7000 years ago, but this date has not yet been firmly established. The people lived in platform villages built on huge dirt mounds along the Amazon floodplains. Some of the mounds held twenty houses. The houses were made of mud, tree trunks, and thatch. These people may have been the first pottery makers in the Americas. Pottery found in their 7000-year-old settlements is believed to be older than pottery found anywhere else in the Americas. The Amazon people had vast trading networks and used the Amazon River and its tributaries as highways. Pieces of their pottery have been found as far west as the Andes.

hollowed-out pumpkin
for drinking vessel

stone figure from
Lake Titicaca in Peru

a reconstructed piece of clay
pottery in the Santarém style,
incised and punctated
1150-1000 years old

66

Chavin temple
cornice stone

The development of pottery was an important milestone in the evolution of prehistoric culture, for it was both fire- and water-proof. Cooking in pottery was a more efficient way to prepare food than older methods. Pottery also made excellent storage containers. Four thousand years ago pottery was widespread throughout the Americas. Some people have suggested that pottery was brought to the Americas by seafaring Africans or Japanese. Careful studies show, however, that there is no scientific basis to suggest that pottery was introduced from anywhere else. The Amazon people were making pottery about as early as the Japanese, and long before Africans were.

Five-thousand-year-old American pottery found at Valdivia, Ecuador, was decorated with symbols or impressions of maize kernels or cobs. Scientists think pottery decorated with corn was used either in preparing maize for eating or for storing the grain.

Chavin bas-relief on
temple in Peru

fragment 5800-3800 years old

VALDIVIA

front and back view
of a 4350-year-old Valdivia figure

early figure sculptures
from Valdivia

pottery shard

pottery shard,
Valdivia period

OLMEC POTTERY FROM VALLEY OF MEXICO

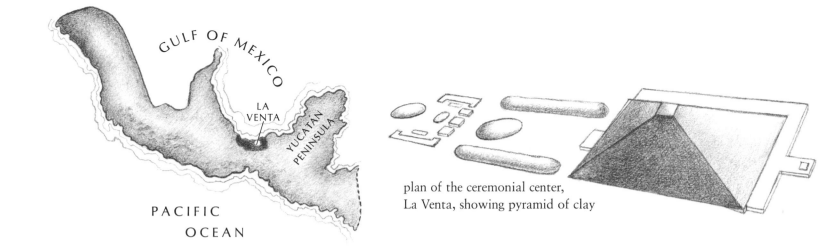

plan of the ceremonial center,
La Venta, showing pyramid of clay

Dried grain was also stored in bell-shaped storage pits, suggesting long-term storage on a community level. Maize was one of the most important food sources of these agricultural people. They cultivated both popcorn and common flint corn.

Other advanced cultures were developing in Mesoamerica by this time. The Olmec culture developed around 3500 years ago along the low-lying Gulf coastal plains. Olmec people traded extensively, spreading their culture into the Mexican highlands and along the western coast. Paintings, drawings, and fragments of pottery of Olmec tradition were found in a cave on the shores of the Pacific Ocean. Olmecs are best known for their monumental sculptures. Huge stone heads were carved from single blocks of basalt that had been quarried miles away. The statues were eight feet (2.4 meters) tall; the largest weighed forty tons. The Olmecs built their major ceremonial city, LaVenta, along the banks of an ancient river. Apparently the river flooded periodically, for traces of long levees built along the riverbank still exist.

Olmec basalt head

buried tomb at La Venta
made of basalt columns

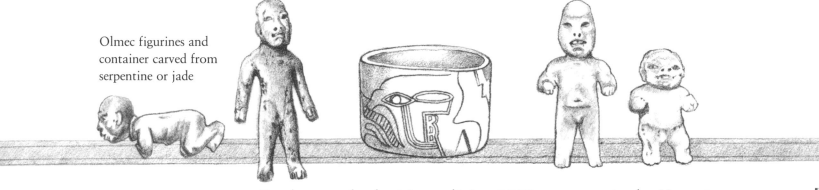

Olmec figurines and container carved from serpentine or jade

Farther south, the Mayas living 3000 years ago in the Yucatán Peninsula were making and trading pottery extensively. By 2500 years ago they were building monumental platforms. These people were accomplished astronomers and had traced the path of Venus with an error of only one day in six thousand years. They developed a calendar as accurate as the one we use today and their mathematicians developed the concept of zero — long before the Arabs thought of it.

Farmers in the Oaxaca (wah-HAH-kah) basin of southwestern Mexico had been growing domesticated crops for a long time. They raised domesticated squash at least 9000 years ago. About 2400 years ago they joined together to create a state or confederation. These people, known as the Zapotecs, carved their capital city, Monte Alban, into the side of a mountain. They built hundreds of terraces on the hillside to hold their palaces, temples, major administrative centers, and homes. They leveled the entire hilltop, an area eight times bigger than St. Peter's Square at the Vatican in Rome, to hold the main plaza. The major buildings were decorated with carved stone slabs. One building contained hieroglyphs — the oldest written text in the Americas — listing the places ruled by the confederation.

Food for the city was grown in the valleys below. The Zapotecs must have spent most of their lives climbing. All supplies — food, water, and raw materials — had to be carried up the mountain on the backs of humans. Nonetheless Monte Alban, a city of at least thirty thousand people, lasted seven hundred years, reaching its peak about 1600 years ago.

Although many people in the Americas were still hunters and gatherers 2000 years ago, many others had adopted more settled ways to live in both small and large communities. Grand empires and nations, rivaling those of the Eastern hemisphere, also arose.

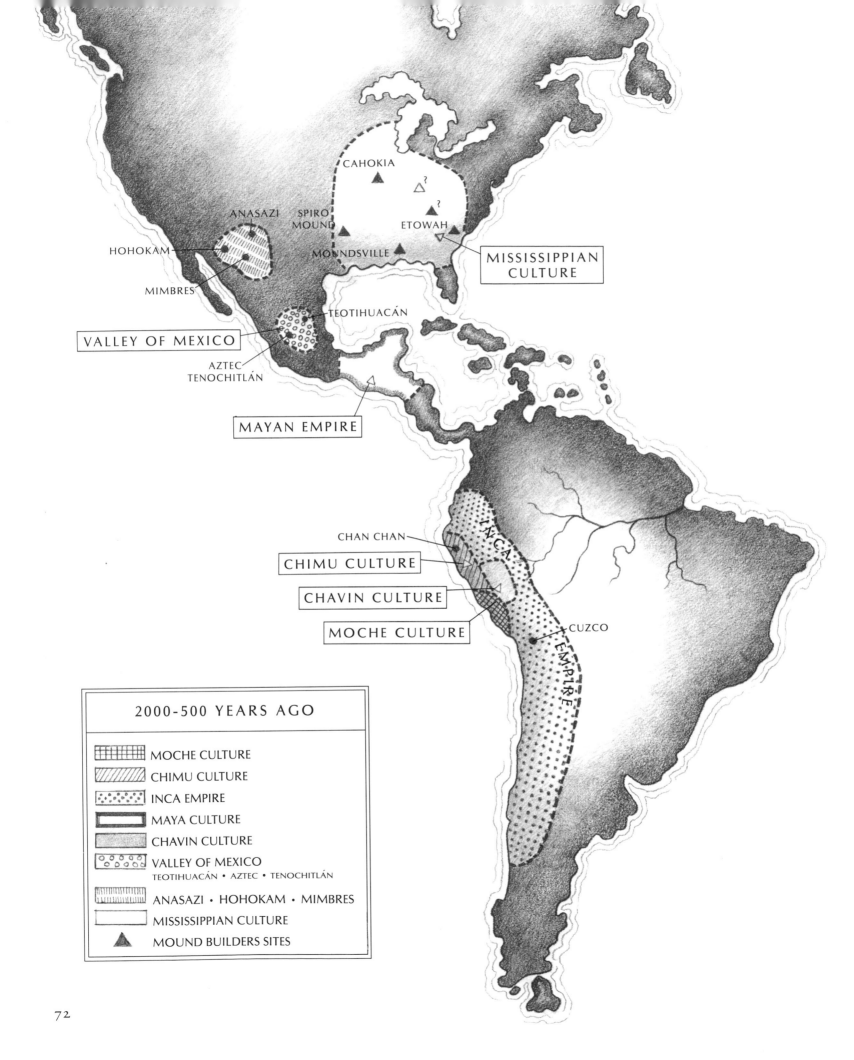

CAHOKIA

ANASAZI   SPIRO
MOUND

HOHOKAM

ETOWAH

MIMBRES

MOUNDSVILLE

MISSISSIPPIAN
CULTURE

TEOTIHUACÁN

VALLEY OF MEXICO

AZTEC
TENOCHITLÁN

MAYAN EMPIRE

CHAN CHAN

INCA

CHIMU CULTURE

CHAVIN CULTURE

MOCHE CULTURE

CUZCO

EMPIRE

2000-500 YEARS AGO

- MOCHE CULTURE
- CHIMU CULTURE
- INCA EMPIRE
- MAYA CULTURE
- CHAVIN CULTURE
- VALLEY OF MEXICO
  TEOTIHUACÁN • AZTEC • TENOCHITLÁN
- ANASAZI • HOHOKAM • MIMBRES
- MISSISSIPPIAN CULTURE
- ▲ MOUND BUILDERS SITES

CHAPTER SEVEN

The Rise of Empires and Nations

2000 TO 500 YEARS AGO

As the populations of early Americans increased and their needs became greater, many of them joined together to form empires and nations. The first of these empires were probably united by religious leaders in areas that had been occupied for long periods of time.

The earliest empire we know about was created by the Moche (MO-chee) in South America around 2000 years ago. About the same time Julius Caesar was forming the Roman Empire in Europe, Moche priests were uniting the city-states of coastal Peru into one of the most remarkable and richest civilizations of the ancient world. Although the Moche left no written records, they told the story of their lives in pictures drawn on pottery vessels and hammered into gold, silver, and copper. These exceptional potters and accomplished metalworkers created beautiful bowls and jewelry for their priests. When their priests died, they placed them, along with all of their possessions, in tombs. The tombs were then covered with huge pyramids made of mud brick. Several of the tombs contained thousands of works of art, jewelry made of gold and silver set with precious gems, and solid gold masks and armor.

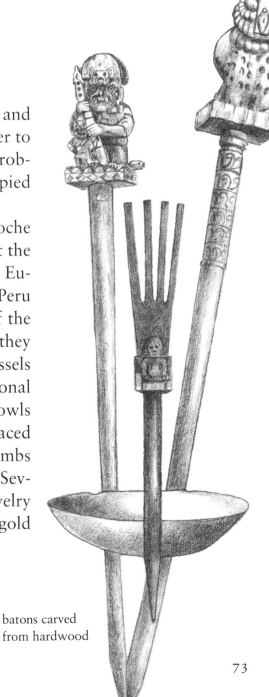

batons carved from hardwood

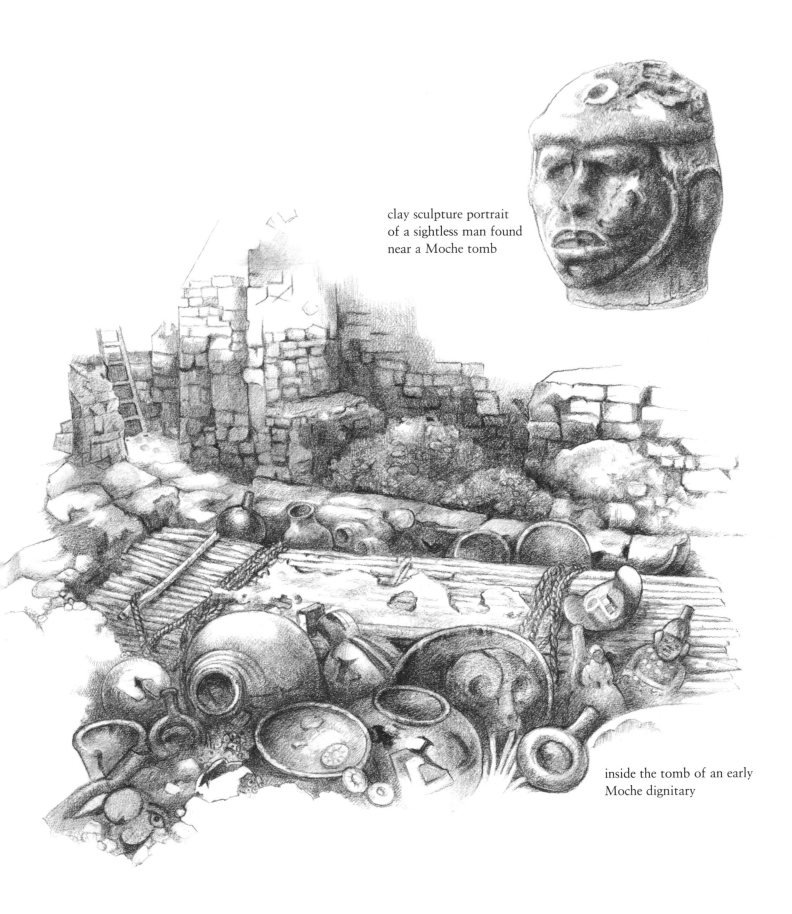

clay sculpture portrait
of a sightless man found
near a Moche tomb

inside the tomb of an early
Moche dignitary

The Moche empire, which was only a little larger than the state of Vermont, was extremely arid, but it supported a population of perhaps 100,000 people. Only seven thousand people can survive in this region today. The resourceful Moche invented methods of irrigation that made it possible to produce crops seven times larger than those of modern farmers. They also domesticated and raised llamas, alpacas, guinea pigs, and ducks for food.

Llamas were also used as pack animals, carrying trading goods in packs slung across their backs. The Moche apparently traded with people in far places. Some of the precious stones used in their jewelry came from Chile, hundreds of miles to the south. Rare seashells came from Ecuador, hundreds of miles to the north. Exotic birds and animals often pictured on their pottery as well as their jewelry came from tropical forests to the north and east.

The Moche empire only lasted about five hundred years. Scientists believe it was destroyed by severe earthquakes followed by torrential rains.

Gold ear ornament,
classic Moche

ceramic blind drummer,
Chimu

ceramic
fish pipe

fish painted on
cotton cloth

wooden
spindle

storage reel
for yarn

A hundred years later another empire with an even more advanced and sophisticated civilization arose along the northwest coast of Peru. This empire, which scientists call the Chimu (CHEE-moo), stretched 1000 miles from southern Ecuador to central Peru. Its capital city was Chan Chan.

Brilliant Chimu engineers built vast networks of earthen and stone-lined aqueducts and canals. Although, as far as we know, the Chimu didn't have a written language, metal tools, or advanced mathematics, they were able to develop methods for distributing water that were not used by Europeans until eight hundred years later. Their only surveying tools were bowls of water and plumb bobs, yet they were able to build aqueducts through mountains and foothills that even modern surveyors would find difficult to cross with canals. These wonderful canals were destroyed by earthquakes several times, but the resourceful Chimu kept rebuilding them. The Chimu empire came to an end about 600 years ago when it was conquered by the Incas.

Inca warrior

The Incas were a talented, ambitious, and warlike people, who by 500 years ago controlled 12 million people living in what is now Peru, Ecuador, Bolivia, and northern Chile. Though they, too, lacked the wheel and iron and never used a written language, their society was nonetheless highly sophisticated. Interestingly, they had developed a written language, but their ruler forbade them to use it because he felt doing so was against the wishes of the gods.

The Inca empire was ruled by powerful monarchs who lived in Cuzco, the capital city. When the Spanish first saw Cuzco, they thought it was as beautiful as any city in Europe. Its palaces and government buildings were made of stone; its temples were faced with gold.

The monarchs were skillful managers. Instead of large, expensive armies, they used food and supplies, politics, and religion to persuade conquered tribes to live peacefully within the vast empire. They built huge storerooms in each city and filled them with textiles, arms, and food to protect the citizens against famine or siege.

an entrance to the Inca city of Machu Picchu

The Inca bound the empire together with an impressive road system. Ten thousand miles of roads stretched from Chile to Colombia and from the Pacific Ocean across the Andes to the Amazon. They were paved with stones set so close together the blade of a knife couldn't be shoved between them. These broad, straight roads were among the finest in the world at the time. Some of them are still in use. Taking the shortest route and using only hand labor, the Incas crossed marshes, lakes, and mountains, building pontoons across lakes and suspension bridges (some 200 feet long) to span chasms, and tunneling through or building steps over steep rock cliffs. The roads fanned out from Cuzco like the spokes of a wheel.

Some scientists think that the roads fanning out from the city may have served as an astronomical calendar because some of them lead to stone markers on hilltops. Even today, when the sun's rays reach these markers, it is time to plant crops.

The roads were also used by pilgrims who came to the city to worship. They traveled the roads on foot because they had no animals strong enough to carry them; horses were extinct throughout the Americas at this time, and they did not have wheeled vehicles. The Incas built lodgings and storehouses every twenty-five miles along the roads for the convenience of travelers. These may have been America's first rest stops and motels.

The Incas had no money to hire laborers. Instead, the rulers levied labor taxes on all of their subjects. Each was required to work a certain amount of time every year to build roads, temples, and government buildings. No one knows how long this impressive empire would have lasted if it had not been conquered by the Spanish.

INCA PERU'S ROAD SYSTEM
—— OLDEST ROADS ---- CONNECTORS

COLOMBIA

ECUADOR

PERU

BRAZIL

this Mayan chocolate jar
had a "lock-top" Rio Azul,
Guatemala 1500 years old

section of a stone tablet
with incised head of Chac,
the Mayan rain god

Mayan glyph for
"chocolate"

Meantime other early Americans were establishing empires in Central America. By 1750 years ago the Maya had united under a single ruler and they became one of the greatest civilizations of the ancient world. They invented a system of writing called glyphics (GLIF-ics), which they used to record the details of the lives of their kings and the dates they ruled. These were carved on the steps of the kings' tombs or on stone tablets inside the tombs. Thus the tombs became permanent history books; some of them were ten stories tall. The Maya also apparently used glyphics to label storage jars and vases. A 1500-year-old ceremonial vase that is decorated with the Mayan symbol for chocolate still contained remnants of chocolate when it was found. By 1200 years ago, the Maya were keeping records in books called codices (co-de-SEES). A Mayan codex was an accordion-folded book made of animal hide and bark.

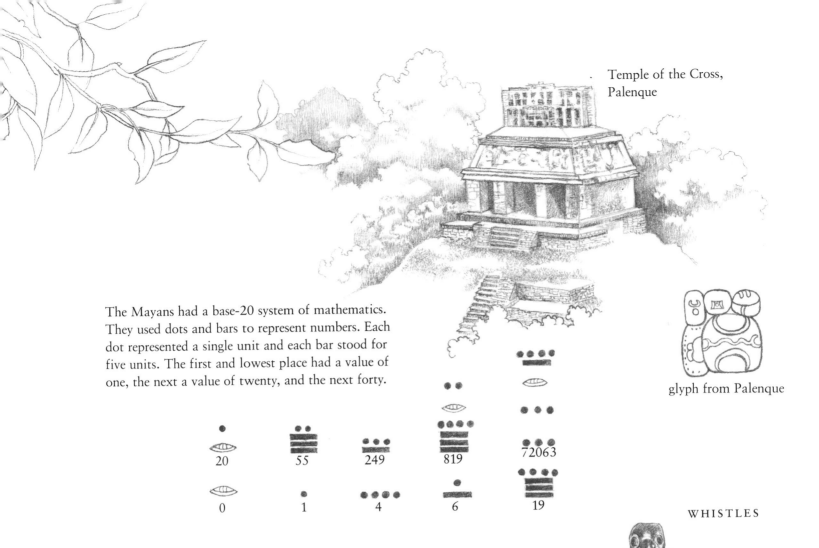

Temple of the Cross, Palenque

glyph from Palenque

The Mayans had a base-20 system of mathematics. They used dots and bars to represent numbers. Each dot represented a single unit and each bar stood for five units. The first and lowest place had a value of one, the next a value of twenty, and the next forty.

20   55   249   819   72063

0   1   4   6   19

The Mayan empire, the greatest pre-Columbian civilization in the Americas, consisted of two hundred cities in southern Mexico, Honduras, Belize, Guatemala, and El Salvador and had a population of 12 to 16 million people. These extremely intelligent and creative people not only used inventiveness to solve the problems of a large society and big government, they also excelled in arts, crafts, science, and mathematics and established special schools taught by priests. They were also talented musicians. All ceremonial occasions were celebrated with drums, whistles, rattles, trumpets, flutes, and maracas.

To provide water during the dry season for cities that had no permanent water supply such as a river or spring, the Maya built large reservoirs to catch rainwater. They also practiced sophisticated forest management. If their methods were used today, the world's tropical rain forests would not be in danger.

WHISTLES

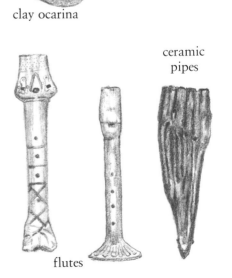

obsidian

clay ocarina

ceramic pipes

flutes

It is not known for sure why the Mayan empire declined. Some scientists suggest the decline was due to overcultivation. Others blame it on invasion or disease. The most recent theory, based on information gleaned from the latest translations of their writings, suggests that the fall of this great civilization was due to increased warfare. The Mayan culture was not only the greatest, but the most violent of the early Americans. The prestige of their rulers was based on power and success in battles. In time, the Mayan wars became so frequent and environmentally destructive that the empire could no longer support itself. Whatever the cause, the empire disappeared around 1200 years ago. The Mayan culture, however, continued, divided into independent city-states, until the arrival of the Spanish in 1519.

About the same time the Moche were building their empire and sometime before the Mayan empire arose, the people in the Valley of Mexico, led by powerful priests, erected the city of Teotihuacán, which means "place to go to worship the gods." Unlike the Maya, with whom they traded, the Teotihuacanos (tay-OH-tih-wah-KAN-oz) did not have a written language. Nonetheless their ceremonial and religious center became the largest pre-Columbian site in the Americas and one of the great cities of the world. The pyramids of the Sun and Moon, which stand in the center of the city, are two of the most impressive man-made monuments in the Americas. The Pyramid of the Sun,

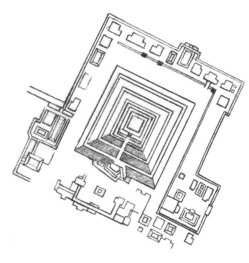

TEOTIHUACÁN

which is larger than the pyramids of Egypt, is 200 feet tall and each side at the base is longer than two football fields. The ceremonial center was surrounded by homes for the priests, and beyond them were the homes of the craftsmen and farmers. Teotihuacán thrived until 1250 years ago. Its impressive pyramids and many of its buildings still stand.

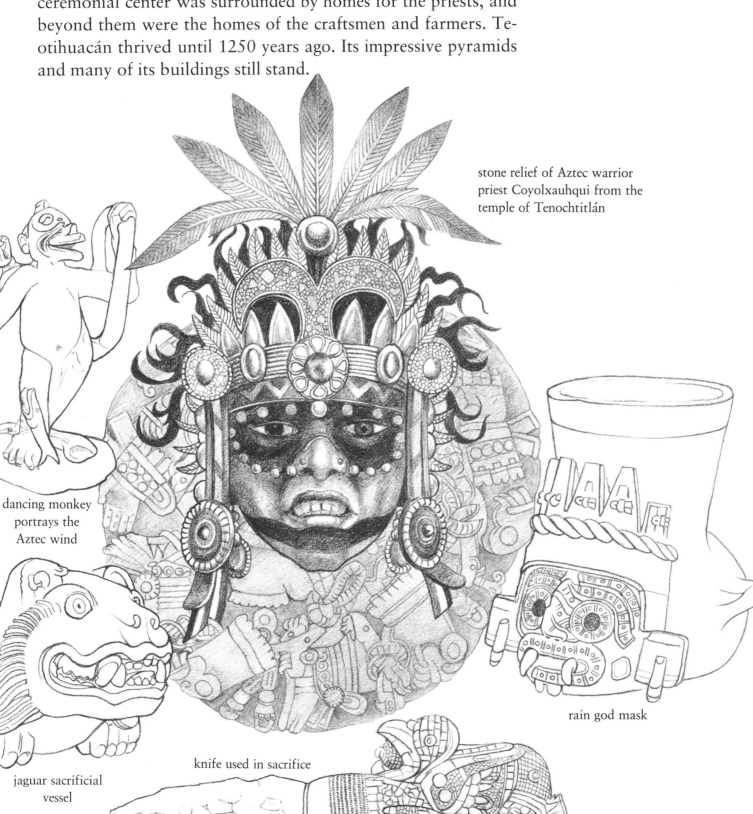

stone relief of Aztec warrior priest Coyolxauhqui from the temple of Tenochtitlán

dancing monkey portrays the Aztec wind

rain god mask

jaguar sacrificial vessel

knife used in sacrifice

VALLEY OF MEXICO

By 500 years ago the Aztec were in control of central Mexico. Their empire stretched from the Pacific Ocean to the Gulf of Mexico and from northern Mexico to Guatemala. The king of these warlike people had absolute power and enforced severe laws. The religion of the Aztec was highly organized and dominated their lives.

Like the Maya, the Aztec set up elaborate school systems staffed by priests and recorded their history in codices. They were highly skilled in metal, pottery, weaving, and stonecutting. They also had a good knowledge of medicine and medicinal use of plants.

Eight hundred years ago, the Aztec built their capital city, Tenochtitlán (tay-NOCH-tih-TLAN), "place of prickly pear cactus," in the swamps of Lake Texcoco, where Mexico City now stands. Tenochtitlán was one of the largest cities in the world, about the same size London was at that time. Two hundred thousand people lived there. All kinds of foods and services could be obtained from its markets. The Aztec were skilled architects, and Tenochtitlán's magnificent palaces and temples made it one of the most beautiful cities in the world before it was conquered by Cortez in 1519.

At the same time empires were flourishing in South America and Mesoamerica, there were other types of advanced civilization centers thriving in the United States.

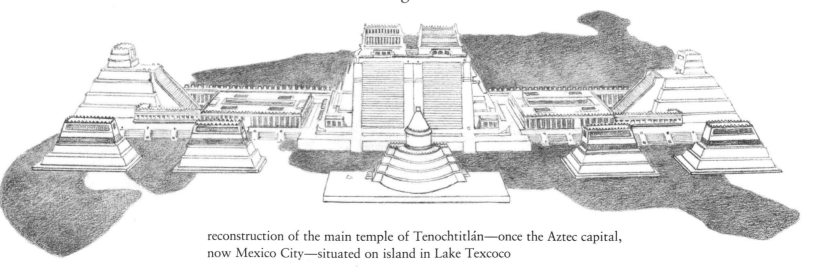

reconstruction of the main temple of Tenochtitlán—once the Aztec capital, now Mexico City—situated on island in Lake Texcoco

CHAPTER EIGHT

The Rise of Nations in the United States

2000 TO 500 YEARS AGO

THE BEST-KNOWN ADVANCED ancient civilization in the United States was created by the Anasazi (an-ah-ZAH-zee) around 1550 years ago, in Chaco Canyon near the Four Corners region of Colorado, Arizona, New Mexico, and Utah. Many ruins of this impressive civilization remain today. In spite of the very arid climate of this area, the Anasazi created a flourishing cultural center a thousand years before Columbus discovered America. They did it using only strong hands, a few simple tools, and a method of agriculture called dry farming that was as good as any method in use today.

By 850 years ago the Anasazi had spread into nearly every livable part of the Colorado plateau. One of the most impressive of these outlying cities was Mesa Verde, Colorado. The Anasazi occupied an area about the size of South Carolina. These remarkable people devised intricate water-control systems with check dams and reservoirs. They built multistoried apartment buildings and a 300-mile road system to seventy-five outlying communities. Some of their roads were thirty feet wide and led to cities ninety miles away.

Mesa Verde

One of their buildings, Pueblo Bonito (which means beautiful house in Spanish), still stands. It was the largest building ever built anywhere up to that time. It was almost twice as wide as a football field and longer than two football fields placed end to end and was four to five stories high. It had 800 rooms. There were dozens of other buildings nearly as large in nearby towns.

The Anasazi used solar energy to heat their homes. Pueblo Bonito was designed to absorb the greatest amount of the sun's radiant energy in winter. Its thick, well-insulated walls prevented heat loss in winter and kept it cool in summer.

Like most early American civilizations, the Anasazi incorporated astronomical alignments into every phase of their lives, including their buildings. Their solar calendars were so accurate they still mark solstices and equinoxes. The Anasazi probably needed precise calendars for determining the best time to plant and harvest.

No one knows for sure why the Anasazi abandoned their empire before the arrival of Europeans. Perhaps it was because they had cut all of the nearby trees and none were left to burn or to build homes with. Perhaps severe drought or invasion by enemies caused them to leave. There is evidence of warfare toward the end as well as of increased drought.

Two other cultural centers that were similar to and at least as great as that of the Anasazi were established by the Hohokam in Arizona and the Mogollon (MO-go-yon) in western New Mexico around 2000 years ago.

bracelet carved
from a seashell

turquoise
thunderbird

ceramic pot
1100-800 years old

pottery figures
2500 years old

carved stone palette

stone arrowheads

The Hohokam's population was somewhere between 100,000 and a million people. They lived in twenty-two cities and fed themselves by building 1000 miles of irrigation canals in a 10,000-square-mile area of the desert. These thirty-foot-wide, seven-foot-deep canals were dug by hand and with sharp sticks. Evidence of them and the ruins of the Hohokam's largest city are buried beneath the present city of Phoenix. The Hohokam domesticated wild grains and invented a process of acid etching to create designs on jewelry five hundred years before the method was used in Europe.

stone incense burner

clay funeral
incense burner

horned toad
etched on shell

The Mogollon built their towns in river valleys. Those in the Mimbres (MEM-brays) Valley were among the largest settlements north of Mexico. Their towns resembled the plan of modern Pueblo villages and were second in size only to the Great Houses of Chaco Canyon. The ruins of Casa Malpais, the largest and most complex Mogollon settlement, still stand near Springerville, Arizona. The largest building, a three-story masonry pueblo containing three hundred rooms, may have been used for religious ceremonies. Although the Mogollon dwellings were smaller than those of Chaco Canyon, there were more of them.

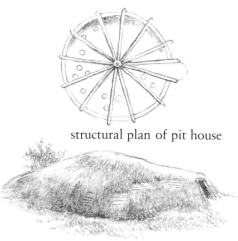

structural plan of pit house

pit house

brushes from yucca leaves

palette

clay

polishing stone

Mimbres Valley
black-and-white
pottery

red and
brown

red

The planning, construction, and maintenance of the irrigation systems in the Mimbres Valley probably required some centralized planning, but archaeologists disagree on how much the Mogollon people used political power for such undertakings. The Mogollon made sandals and rope from plant fiber. They knew all the knots we know — square knot, granny, slip, half hitch, and sheet bend knot. They raised popcorn and popped it on the cob. Until recently, the Mimbres were best known for their exquisite black on white pottery.

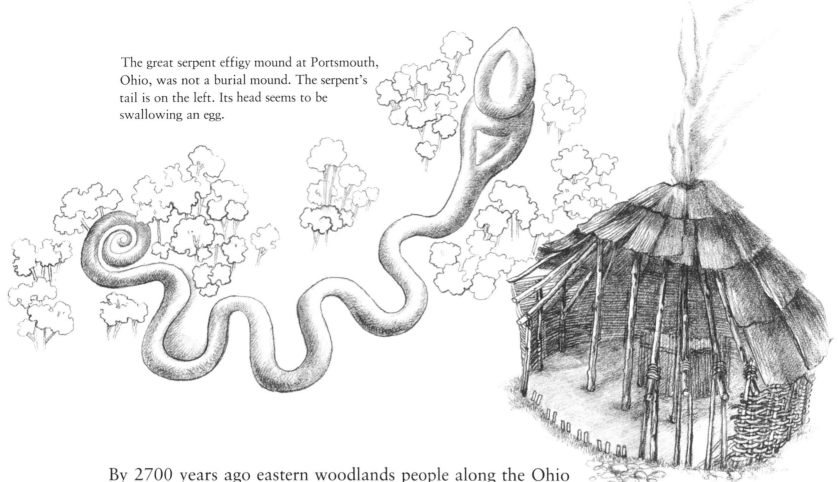

The great serpent effigy mound at Portsmouth, Ohio, was not a burial mound. The serpent's tail is on the left. Its head seems to be swallowing an egg.

reconstruction of an early Adena homestead

By 2700 years ago eastern woodlands people along the Ohio River were living in flourishing villages. In their society, which is known as the Adena (ah-DEE-nah) culture, everyone was considered equal. Their population had grown too large for the wild food supply and they began cultivating squash, pumpkins, sunflowers, and some local plants. Their chiefs and other people of high status were buried with all their possessions. Their graves were covered by high, narrow ridges of earth in the form of circles, squares, or pentagons, which grew over time as other bodies were added to the top.

The Adena culture flourished until 1800 years ago when it was replaced by the Hopewell culture. This culture spread rapidly from Kansas to the Appalachians and from the Canadian border to the Gulf of Mexico. It was a well-organized society led by an elite upper class and had a loose federation of tribes. The Hopewell lived on a grander scale than the Adena. Their burial mounds were bigger and more elaborate. One of the largest (Crook's Mound in Lousiana) is 40 feet tall and 100 feet across.

Adena vase

nine-inch Adena figure carved of florite from Indiana mound

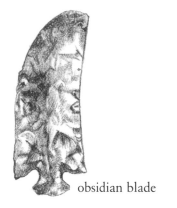

obsidian blade

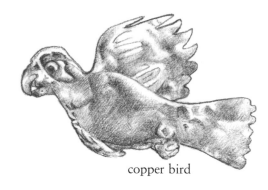

copper bird

flint point

mica bird's claw found
in burial mound

The Hopewell had more luxury items and finer jewelry than the Adena. They controlled vast trading networks. They got obsidian from the Rocky Mountains and traded some of it for copper from Lake Superior, which they made into axes, arrowheads, and jewelry. They also made jewelry from conch shells obtained from the Gulf Coast and mica from the southern Appalachians.

It is unknown why this culture declined around 1400 years ago, perhaps because another center of civilization known as the Mississippian culture sprang up about 1300 years ago along the Mississippi River and its tributaries. These people began growing corn, and their population increased dramatically. Their culture stretched from Louisiana to Wisconsin and from Oklahoma to Ohio, Tennessee, and Alabama.

MONK'S MOUND

1800-year-old Hopewell effigy pipe
carved from steatite

ornaments found in Hopewell mounds

large mound of
Etowah group

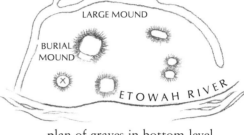

plan of graves in bottom level
of a mound in Etowah group

A huge earthen mound, called Monk's Mound, stands outside East St. Louis, Illinois. This and hundreds of smaller mounds surrounding Monk's Mound are all that remain of Cahokia, the hub and religious center of one nation of the Mississippian culture.

The Adena, Hopewell, and Mississippians are known as the Mound Builders because of the many mounds they left behind. Other important Mississippian sites include Spiro in Oklahoma, Moundsville in Alabama, and Etowah in Georgia.

Monk's Mound is the largest ancient earthen mound in the United States. It covered sixteen acres and was 100 feet tall. The home of the chief probably stood on top of it. The surrounding mounds held temples, burials, and residences of officials. The mound area was defended by a fifteen-foot wooden stockade.

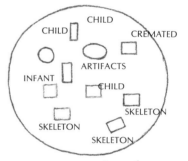

cutaway view of
burial mound above

carved shell gorget
(a piece of armor for
the throat), Etowah

shell carving,
Oklahoma Mississippian

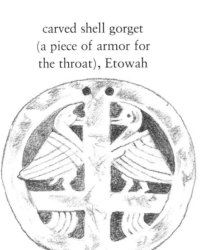

bowl carved from green diorite,
Alabama mound

Nine hundred years ago, Cahokia was a busy, well-organized city of about 30,000 people. Homes of farmers and specialists in arts and crafts were clustered outside the stockade.

Scientists found evidence of huge cedar posts that had been set in perfect circles. They call these circles "woodhenges" because they think the Cahokians used them for astronomical observations. Perhaps the Cahokians used them to determine when to plant corn and when to conduct religious ceremonies. The economy of these highly intelligent people was dependent upon corn. Thousands of the flint hoes used to cultivate the grain were found in the city. Trade was also an important part of their economy. Cahokians traded corn and other goods with people from all over. They were clever merchants, trading goods received from people around the Gulf of Mexico to people from the Great Lakes region and from the Atlantic Coast to the Pacific Coast.

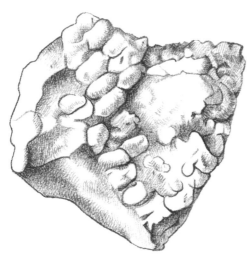

clay cast of maize from hearth in ruins of mound dwelling, Arkansas

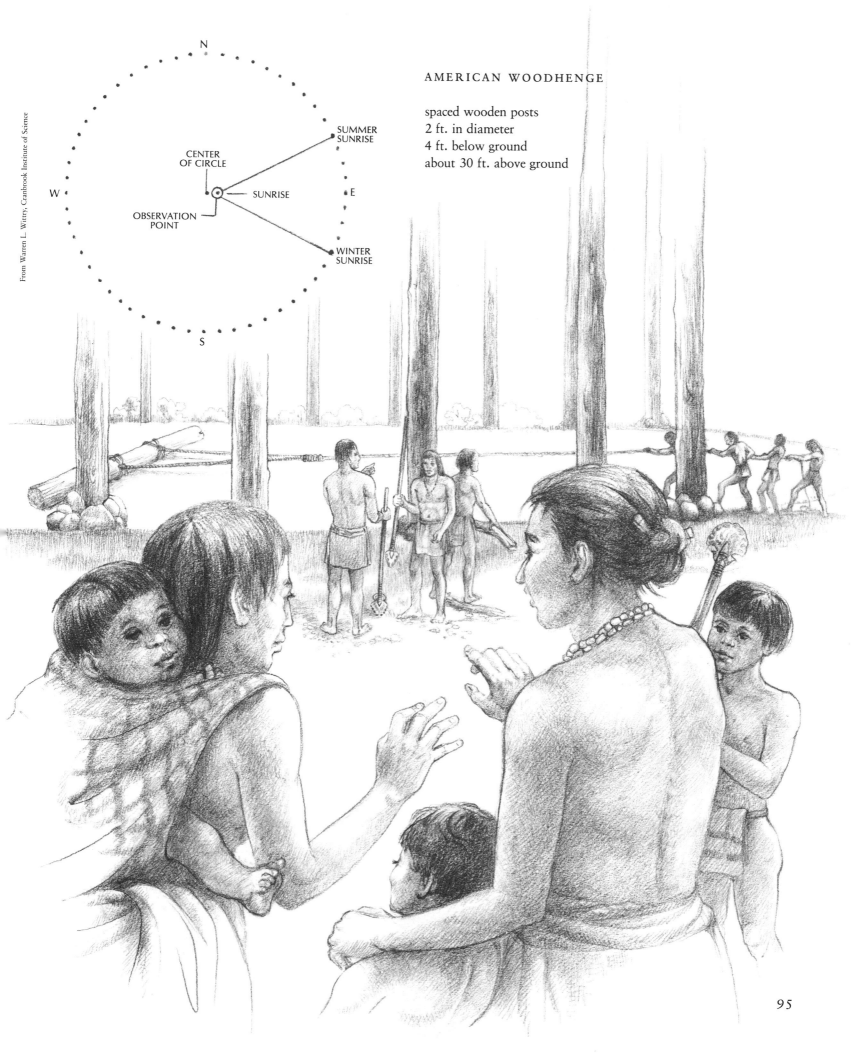

AMERICAN WOODHENGE

spaced wooden posts
2 ft. in diameter
4 ft. below ground
about 30 ft. above ground

N

W

E

S

SUMMER
SUNRISE

CENTER
OF CIRCLE

SUNRISE

OBSERVATION
POINT

WINTER
SUNRISE

From Warren L. Wittry, Cranbrook Institute of Science

95

cave painting, Altimira, Spain
17,000 years ago

cave painting, Lascaux, France
17,000 years ago

Pedra Furada, Brazil
between 12,000-6000 years ago

part of petroglyph, Chaco Canyon
1600 years ago

Almost everything we know about the people of the Americas before Columbus is the result of archaeological fieldwork and study. Often, the greatest breakthroughs in our knowledge occur where and when they are least expected. A recent excavation uncovered charcoal, chipped stones, and what may be a human palm print in Orogrande Cave, New Mexico, tentatively dated at 30,000 years ago. Each discovery gives us new information and insights on the lives of the earliest Americans.

The first ancient catacombs reported in the United States were discovered in 1990 by archaeologists making a routine investigation of the Casa Malpais ruins for the town of Springerville, Arizona. The town hoped to develop the fifteen-acre ruins as a recreational area and was required by law to have an archaeological survey made before permits could be issued. The catacombs had been made from natural fissures that were excavated by the Mogollon people 800 to 700 years ago. The vast underground complex included tombs and hundreds of graves, along with huge, elaborate ceremonial chambers. This astonishing discovery may be one of the most important new sources of knowledge about early people of the American Southwest.

The discovery of the Casa Malpais catacombs also proves the importance of laws that require professional archaeological surveys of land before new developments can begin. It is probable that there are many more equally important sites waiting to reveal their secrets about the lives of ancient Americans.

Although much still remains to be learned about the earliest Americans, some things are clear. They came from Asia. The few tools and other artifacts so far discovered reveal them to have been people with skills as highly developed as those of any other people on earth at the time.

Greek head
2650
years old

Olmec head
2650 years old

Paleo-Arctic hunters and gatherers
Stone Age, 40,000-12,000 years ago

The early Americans, like other ancient people, based their values on close family ties and strong religious beliefs. They learned from their experiences and taught what they learned to their children. The environment shaped their lives. When it changed, they invented new ways to support themselves. Sixty percent of all the domesticated plants used throughout the world today were first domesticated by early Native Americans. Their progress through the centuries is very much like that of people all over the world.

Pedra Furada Rock-shelter, Brazil
17,000 years ago

Monte Verde, Chile
13,000 years ago

Mesa Verde, CO
1081-870 years ago

This long count date (9.1.1.10.10.4)
painted on the wall of a tomb chamber at
Tikal translates March 18, 457 A.D.
The glyphs alongside the date probably describe
the person buried there.

9

1

1

10

10

4

Temple of the
Giant Jaguar, Tikal

glyph of ruler, Double Comb, heir
of the sky dynasty, buried below
temple in vaulted tomb

glyph, Tikal

Until recent times, most people of the world lived in small settlements, as did Native Americans, though there were some large, amazingly sophisticated cities in both hemispheres.

Early American industry included farming, irrigation, arts and crafts, architecture, and trade. Without the use of metal tools or large draft animals early Americans created civilizations that astounded the first Europeans to see them. Insofar as we know, they also made these accomplishments without using the wheel as a tool, though they did know about the wheel. Wheeled pull toys have been found throughout Mesoamerica. As elsewhere in the world, empires and nations developed, flourished for a time, then waned. Some cultures had written languages and mathematics. Almost all were accomplished astronomers.

Progress in the Americas was sometimes set back by wars, diseases, and natural disasters such as drought, flood, earthquakes, and volcanic action. From the hunting and gathering bands that first entered Beringia with their simple stone and bone tools to the glories of Teotihuacán with its Pyramid of the Sun, the long history of human accomplishment on these continents bears witness to the intelligence, creativity, and inventiveness of the earliest Americans.

girl on swing, toy

copy of one-third page
from Madrid codex

dog   deer or dog   cayman

WHEELED TOYS FROM MEXICO

TIME CHART

Years Ago	Americas	Europe	Asia	Africa
40,000	Modern humans. Stone Age hunter-gatherers first American immigrants (?)	Modern humans. Stone Age hunter-gatherers.	Modern humans. Stone Age hunter-gatherers along ice sheet.	Modern humans. Stone Age hunter-gatherers.
36,000	Ft. Bliss, N.M. (?)			
34,000	Monte Verde, Chile (?)			
32,000	Pedra Furada, Brazil (?)			
26,000	Burnham site, Oklahoma.			
25,000	Pikimachay, Peru.			
22,000	Jayamachay, Peru. Ecuador. Colombia. Valsequillo and Tlapacoya, Valley of Mexico (decorated bones).			
20,000	Selby and Dutton, Colorado.			20,000(?)–8000, rock paintings by the San peoples in southern Africa.
19,600	Meadowcroft Rock-shelter, Pennsylvania (basket weaving).			
17,000–14,000	Pedra Furada, Brazil (first rock painting in Americas).	Cave paintings in Europe.		
15,800	Trail Creek, Alaska.			
15,000	Bluefish Cave, Yukon.			
13,000	Taima-Taima, Venezuela (oldest houses in Americas at Monte Verde).			
12,500	Clovis people.			
11,000	Folsom people. Marmes Rock-shelter (oldest North American skeletons).			
10,500	Fell's Cave, Tierra del Fuego.		Farming. Domesticated sheep. Domesticated wheat and barley in Fertile Crescent. Civilization in Mesopotamia.	

Years Ago	Americas	Europe	Asia	Africa
10,000	Sierra Nevada Mountains (oldest house in United States).			Domesticated cattle in eastern Sahara. Bow and arrow.
9000	Domesticated squash in Mexico. Bow and arrow in Utah.			
8500	Domesticated peppers and gourds (agriculture) in Peru.			
8000	Mummies in coastal Peru.	Civilization. Farming (agriculture). Domesticated wheat, barley, cattle, sheep, goats.	Pottery in Near East. Cities in Mesopotamia.	Domesticated barley (agriculture).
7000	Andes Highlands culture. Amazonia (first American pottery). Domesticated maize (corn) and beans.	Widespread trade. Pottery.	Domesticated rice, pig, water buffalo. Metal tools in China. Trade networks. Sumerian city-states in Fertile Crescent, Mesopotamia. Agriculture in India. Domesticated horse. Use of wheel.	Pottery in Nile Valley. Houses in Nile Valley.
6000		Copper metallurgy.		
6500	Red Paint People, northeastern seacoast (first burial mounds).			
5500	Domesticated llamas in Peru (first domesticated animals in America).	City of Troy.		5600, metallurgy in Nile Valley.
5400			Writing and copper weights in Crescent Valley.	
5200				Seagoing ships in East Africa. Cities in Egypt.
5000	Deep-sea fishing off coast of Maine.	High civilization in Aegean Islands.	Trade in Sumer. Bronze Age.	High civilization in Egypt. First pharaohs, First Empire. Metallurgy. Earliest hieroglyphics.
4800	First pyramids in Peru.		Cities of 10,000–15,000 population, Indus Valley civilization.	

Years Ago	Americas	Europe	Asia	Africa
4600	Aspero, Peru.	Bow and arrow.		Pyramid age in Egypt. Ca. 4680, first pyramid built.
4500	First maize cultivation. El Paraíso, Peru.	4300, Bronze Age in Greece.	Chinese civilization. Trade networks.	Pyramids of Giza.
4000	Pottery widespread. Irrigation in Peru.	Stonehenge, England. Minoan civilization.	Abraham leads Hebrews to Canaan. Hammurabi Empire, Babylonia. Mud bricks.	Egyptian calendar.
3800		Bronze Age throughout Europe.		
3700	Canal system in Peru.			
3600		First cities in Europe.	Phoenicians invent alphabet.	
3500	Olmec culture in Mexico.	Mycenaean civilization.		
3400			Hittites have iron.	
3200	Rise of Olmec culture in Central America. Cities.	Iron Age in Europe.	Bronze in Indus Valley. Bow and arrow in China.	
3000	Tiwanaku, Bolivia, city of 40,000 population.	Urnfield peoples working bronze in Po Valley.	David rules Kingdom of Judah. Domesticated camel.	
2900				Meroe people trading and ironworking in area of Sudan.
2800	Chavin culture in Peru.	Rise of Greek civilization.		
2700	Adena culture, trading widely, in area of Ohio River Valley.			
2600			Nebuchadnezzar conquers Jerusalem.	
2500	Mayan culture expands. Calendar. Math, concept of zero. Astronomy.	Greek city-states.	Buddhism founded in India.	Persian conquest of Middle East, Egypt, and Thrace.
2400	Monte Alban, Mexico, earliest known complex society in Americas. Hieroglyphs.	Alexander the Great rises to power.	Weights and measures in China.	Conquest of Egypt and Persian Empire by Alexander the Great.
2300		Roman Empire emerging.		Ironworking in West Africa.
2200	Teotihuacán, Mexico, 125,000 population.			

Years Ago	Americas	Europe	Asia	Africa
2100	Hohokam and Mogollon in United States.			
2000 A.D. 1	Moche culture empire in Peru. Metallurgy. Adena culture.		Jesus born in Bethlehem.	
1900 A.D. 100		Julius Caesar. Roman Empire at its height.	Paper invented in China.	Papyrus paper and ink invented in Egypt.
1800 A.D. 200	Hopewell culture.			
1700–900 A.D. 300	Maya empire. Hieroglyphs, codices, chocolate.		Constantine the Great rules, 312–337.	
1600 A.D. 400		Fall of Roman Empire.		
1550 A.D. 450	Anasazi culture in United States.			
1500 A.D. 500	Chimu, Peru.			
1400 A.D. 600			Islam founded in Arabia.	
1300 A.D. 700	Mississippian culture and Mound Builders.			
1200 A.D. 800		Charlemagne crowned first Holy Roman Emperor.		
1000 A.D. 1000		Norsemen visit America. Leif Ericson names it Vinland.	Earliest book printed in Korea.	Powerful kingdoms develop in central and southern Africa.
930 A.D. 1070	Cahokia culture at its peak.	Norman Conquest of England, 1066. Crusades begin, 1096.		Kingdom of Ghana.
800 A.D. 1200	Inca empire in Peru. Bronze metallurgy.	Magna Carta, 1215.	Genghis Khan invades China and conquers Persia.	Kingdom of Mali founded by Sundiata.
729 A.D. 1271		Marco Polo of Venice travels to China.	Kublai Khan rules China.	
650 A.D. 1350	Aztec empire of ca. one million people flourishing in Mexico. Estimated Native American population ca. 30–40 million.	Bubonic plague, 25 million people die, 1347–1351.	Ming Dynasty begins, 1368.	Mali Empire reaches its height under King Mansa Munsa.
500 A.D. 1500	Columbus lands on American shores, Oct. 12, 1492.	Columbus sails west from Palos, Spain, in search of a new route to India, Aug. 3, 1492.		

Bibliography

1. Where the First Americans Came From

Anderson, Douglas D. "A Stone Age Campsite at the Gateway to America." In *Readings from Scientific American: New World Archaeology*. San Francisco: W. H. Freeman and Company, 1974, 61–70.

Boellstorff, John. "North American Pleistocene Stages Reconsidered in Light of Probable Pliocene-Pleistocene Continental Glaciation." *Science,* October 20, 1978, 305–7.

Bower, B. "People in the Americas Before the Last Ice Age?" *Science News,* June 28, 1986, 405–6.

———. "Marine Scene Expands for Early Americans." *Science News,* March 12, 1988, 164.

———. "Promising New Clues to Early Americans." *Science News,* April 23, 1988, 261.

———. "Asian Human-Origin Theory Gets New Teeth." *Science News,* August 12, 1989, 100.

———. "Common Origin Cited for American Indians." *Science News,* August 4, 1990, 68.

Canby, Thomas Y. "The Search for the First Americans." *National Geographic,* September 1979, 330–63.

Colinvaux, Paul A. "Bering Land Bridge: Evidence of Spruce in Late-Wisconsin Times." *Science,* April 21, 1967, 380–83.

Cotter, John L. "Human Habitation of the Americas." *Science,* October 5, 1990, 14.

Dikow, Nikolai N. "On the Road to America." *Natural History,* January 1988, 10–14.

Emiliani, Cesare. "Ice Sheets and Ice Melts." *Natural History,* November 1980, 88–91.

Fagan, Brian M. *The Great Journey: The Peopling of Ancient America.* New York: Thames and Hudson, 1987.

———. *People of the Earth: An Introduction to World Prehistory,* 199–252. 6th ed. New York: HarperCollins Publishers, 1989.

Fladmark, Knut R. "Times and Places: Environmental Correlates of Mid-to-Late Wisconsinian Human Population Expansion in North America." In *Early Man in the New World,* 13–42. Beverly Hills, California: Sage Publications, 1983.

Gallant, Roy A. "Who Were the First Americans?" *Science 81,* April 1981, 94–96.

———. *Ancient Indians, the First Americans.* Hillside, New Jersey: Enslow Publishers, 1989.

Garret, Wilbur E. "Where Did We Come From?" *National Geographic,* October 1988, 434–37.

Hanihara, Kazuro. "Dental Traits in Ainu, Australian Aborigines, and New World Populations." In *The First Americans: Origins, Affinities, and Adaptations,* 125–34. New York: Gustav Fischer, 1979.

Haynes, C. Vance, Jr. "The Earliest Americans." *Science,* November 7, 1969, 709–15.

Hopkins, David M. "Landscape and Climate of Beringia During Late Pleistocene and Holocene Time." In *The First Americans: Origins, Affinities, and Adaptations,* 15–41. New York: Gustav Fischer, 1979.

Kukla, George J. "Around the Ice Age World." *Natural History,* April 1976, 56–61.

Laughlin, William S. "Aleuts: Ecosystems, Holocene History, and Siberian Origin." *Science,* August 13, 1975, 507–15.

Laughlin, William S., and Albert B. Harper. *The First Americans: Origins, Affinities, and Adaptations.* New York: Gustav Fischer, 1979.

Lewin, Roger. "Speaking in Many Tongues." *Science,* November 27, 1987, 1232.

———. "American Indian Language Dispute." *Science,* December 23, 1988, 1632–33.

Martin, Paul. "The Discovery of America." *Science,* March 9, 1973, 969–74.

Ruhlem, Merritt. "Voices of the Past." *Natural History,* March 1987, 6–10.

Schull, William J., and Francisco Rothhammer. "Analytic Methods for Genetic and Adaptational Studies." In *The First Americans: Origins, Affinities, and Adaptations,* 241–55. New York: Gustav Fischer, 1979.

Schwert, Donald P., and Allan C. Ashworth. "Ice Age Beetles." *Natural History,* January 1990, 10–14.

Shutler, Richard, Jr., ed. *Early Man in the New World.* Beverly Hills, California: Sage Publications, 1983.

———. "The Australian Parallel to the Peopling of the New World." In

Early Man in the New World, 43–46. Beverly Hills, California: Sage Publications, 1983.

Stewart, T. Dale. "Patterning of Skeletal Pathologies and Epidemiology." In *The First Americans: Origins, Affinities, and Adaptations,* 257–74. New York: Gustav Fischer, 1979.

Turner, Christy G., II. "Dental Evidence for Peopling of the Americas." In *Early Man in the New World,* 147–58. Beverly Hills, California: Sage Publications, 1983.

———. "Telltale Teeth." *Natural History,* January 1987, 6–10.

———. "Teeth and Prehistory in Asia." *Scientific American,* February 1989, 88–96.

Zubrow, Ezra B. W., Margret C. Fritz, and John M. Fritz, eds. *Readings from Scientific American: New World Archaeology.* San Francisco: W. H. Freeman and Company, 1974.

2. Paleo-Indians in Beringia

Aigner, Jean. "Early Arctic Settlements in North America." *Scientific American,* November 1985, 160–69.

Baba, Jeffrey I., Roy A. Schroeder, and George F. Carter. "New Evidence for the Antiquity of Man in North America Deduced from Aspartic Acid Racemization." *Science,* May 17, 1974, 791–93.

Berger, Rainer. "New Dating Techniques." In *Early Man in the New World,* 159–62. Beverly Hills, California: Sage Publications, 1983.

Bischoff, James, and Robert J. Rosenbauer. "Uranium Series Dating of Human Skeletal Remains from the DelMar and Sunnyvale Sites, California." *Science,* August 28, 1981, 1003–5.

Bray, Warwick. "Finding the Earliest Americans." *Nature,* June 19, 1986, 726.

Canby, Thomas Y. "The Search for the First Americans." *National Geographic,* September 1979, 330–63.

Dumond, Don E. "The Archeology of Alaska and the Peopling of America." *Science,* August 29, 1980, 984–91.

Fagan, Brian M. *The Great Journey: The Peopling of Ancient America.* New York: Thames and Hudson, 1987.

———. *People of the Earth: An Introduction to World Prehistory,* 199–232. 6th ed. New York: HarperCollins Publishers, 1989.

Fladmark, Knut R. "Getting One's Berings." *Natural History,* November 1986, 8–19.

Giddings, J. L. "First Traces of Man in the Arctic." *Natural History,* November 1960, 8–19.

———. "Cross-Dating the Archeology of Northwestern Alaska." *Science,* July 8, 1966, 127–35.

———. "Early Man in the Arctic." In *Readings from Scientific American: New World Archaeology,* 92–96. San Francisco: W. H. Freeman and Company, 1974.

Griffin, James B. "The Origin and Dispersion of American Indians in North America." In *The First Americans: Origins, Affinities, and Adaptations,* 43–55. New York: Gustav Fischer, 1979.

Haag, William G. "The Bering Strait Land Bridge." In *Readings from Scientific American: New World Archaeology,* 263–70. San Francisco: W. H. Freeman and Company, 1974.

Haynes, Vance. "Geofacts and Fancy." *Natural History,* February 1988, 4–12.

Hopkins, David M. "Landscape and Climate of Beringia During Late Pleistocene and Early Holocene Time." In *The First Americans: Origins, Affinities, and Adaptations,* 15–41. San Francisco: W. H. Freeman and Company, 1974.

Irving, William N. "New Dates from Old Bones." *Natural History,* February 1987, 8–13.

Irving, William N. and C. R. Harinton. "Upper Pleistocene Radiocarbon-Dated Artefacts from the Northern Yukon." *Science,* January 26, 1973, 335–40.

Kukla, George J. "Around the Ice Age World." *Natural History,* April 1976, 56–61.

Lanning, Edward P., and Thomas C. Patterson. "Early Man in South America." In *Readings from Scientific American: New World Archaeology,* 44–50. San Francisco: W. H. Freeman and Company, 1974.

Laughlin, William S., Jorgen B. Jorgensen, and Bruno Frohlich. "Aleuts and Eskimos: Survivors of the Bering Land Bridge Coast." In *The First Americans: Origins, Affinities, and Adaptations,* 91–104. New York: Gustav Fischer, 1979.

Lewin, Roger. "The First Americans Are Getting Younger." *Science,* November 27, 1987, 1230–32.

MacNeish, Richard S. "Mesoamerica." In *Readings from Scientific American: New World Archaeology,* 125–36. San Francisco: W. H. Freeman and Company, 1974.

Morlan, Richard E. "Pre-Clovis Occupation North of the Ice Sheets." In *Early Man in the New World,* 47–64. Beverly Hills, California: Sage Publications, 1983.

Muller-Beck, Hansjurgen. "Paleohunters in America: Origins and Diffusion." *Science,* May 27, 1966, 1191–1210.

Park, Edwards. "The Ginsberg Caper: Hacking It as in Stone Age." *Smithsonian,* July 1978, 85–86.

Patton, William W., Jr., and Thomas P. Miller. "A Possible Bedrock Source for Obsidian Found in Archeological Sites in Northwestern Alaska." *Science,* August 21, 1970, 760–61.

Schwert, Donald P., and Allan C. Ashworth. "Ice Age Beetles." *Natural History,* January 1990, 10–14.

Stanford, Dennis, Robson Bonnichsen, and Richard E. Morlan. "The Ginsberg Experiment: Modern and Prehistoric Evidence of a Bone-Flaking Technology." *Science,* April 24, 1981, 438–39.

Wardwell, Allen. "Ancient Eskimo Ivories of the Bering Strait." *Archaeology*, July/August 1986, 54–57.

3. Beyond Beringia

Bower, B. "Skeletal Aging of the New World Settlers." *Science News*, April 22, 1988, 215.

Bray, Warwick. "Finding the Earliest Americans." *Nature*, June 19, 1986, 726.

Bryan, Alan L. "South America." In *Early Man in the New World*, 137–48. Beverly Hills, California: Sage Publications, 1983.

Bryan, Alan L., and others. "An El Jobo Mastodon Kill at Taima-Taima, Venezuela." *Science*, June 16, 1986, 1275–77.

Canby, Thomas Y. "The Search for the First Americans." *National Geographic*, September 1979, 330–63.

Coe, Michael D. "Post-Pleistocene Foragers." *Science*, September 12, 1986, 1207.

Diamond, Jared. "The Latest on the Earliest." *Discover*, January 1990, 50.

Dillehay, Tom D. "A Late Ice-Age Settlement in Southern Chile." *American Scientist*, October 1984, 106–17.

———. "By the Banks of the Chinchihuapi." *Natural History*, April 1987, 8–12.

Fagan, Brian M. *The Great Journey: The Peopling of Ancient America*. New York: Thames and Hudson, 1987.

Gay, Carlo T. E. "Oldest Paintings in the New World." *Natural History*, April 1967, 28–35.

Guidon, Niedon. "Cliff Notes: Rock Artists May Have Left Mark in Brazil More Than 30,000 Years Ago." *Natural History*, August 1987, 6–12.

Guidon, Niedon, and G. Delibrias. "Carbon-14 Dates Point to Man in the Americas 32,000 Years Ago." *Nature*, June 19, 1986, 769–71.

Haynes, C. Vance, Jr. "The Earliest Americans." *Science*, November 7, 1969, 709–15.

———. "Early Man Site Visits." *Science*, November 10, 1989, 9.

"How to Date a Rock Artist." *Science*, January 19, 1991, 45.

Lange, Fredrick W. "Prehistory in the Tropics." *Science*, March 27, 1981, 1412–13.

Lanning, Edward P., and Thomas C. Patterson. "Early Man in South America." In *Readings from Scientific American: New World Archaeology*. San Francisco: W. H. Freeman and Company, 1974.

Lewin, Roger. "Flake Tools Stratified Below Paleo-Indian Artifacts." *Science*, June 16, 1978, 1272–72.

———. "Skepticism Fades Over Pre-Clovis Man." *Science*, June 9, 1989, 1140.

Lister, Robert H. "Archeology for Layman and Scientist at Mesa Verde." *Science*, May 3, 1968, 489–96.

Lynch, Thomas F., and Kenneth A. R. Kennedy. "Early Human Cultural and Skeletal Remains from Guitarrero Cave, Northern Peru." *Science*, September 25, 1970, 1307–9.

Mayer-Oakes, William J. "Early Man in the Andes." In *Readings from Scientific American: New World Archaeology*. San Francisco: W. H. Freeman and Company, 1974.

Muller-Beck, Hansjurgen. "Paleohunters in America: Origins and Diffusion." *Science*, May 27, 1966, 1191–1210.

Osborne, Douglas. "Slow Exodus from Mesa Verde." *Natural History*, January 1976, 38–45.

4. Paleo-Indians in North America

Adovasio, J. M., and Ronald C. Carlisle. "Pennsylvania Pioneers." *Natural History*, December 1986, 20–27.

———. "The Meadowcroft Rockshelter." *Science*, February 12, 1988, 713.

Adovasio, J. M., and others. "Evidence from Meadowcroft Rockshelter." In *Early Man in the New World*, 163–90. Beverly Hills, California: Sage Publications, 1983.

Ahler, Stanley A., and others. "Holocene Stratigraphy and Archeology in the Middle Missouri River Trench, South Dakota." *Science*, May 24, 1974, 905–7.

Barajas, Anne. "Survey Keeping Low-Key About Controversial Archaeological Find." *O. U. Update*, July 12, 1989, 13.

Borden, Charles E. "Peopling and Early Cultures of the Pacific Northwest." *Science*, March 9, 1979, 963–71.

Carlson, Roy L. "The Far West." In *Early Man in the New World*, 73–96. Beverly Hills, California: Sage Publications, 1983.

"Early Man Site in California to Be Preserved." *Archaeological Conservancy Newsletter*, Summer 1987.

Fagan, Brian M. *The Great Journey: The Peopling of Ancient America*. New York: Thames and Hudson, 1987.

———. *People of the Earth: An Introduction to World Prehistory*, 199–232. 6th ed. New York: HarperCollins Publishers, 1989.

Haynes, C. Vance, Jr. "The Earliest Americans." *Science*, November 7, 1969, 709–15.

———. "Geofacts and Fancy." *Natural History*, February 1988, 4–12.

Haynes, C. Vance, Jr., and Thomas E. Hemmings. "Mammoth-Bone Shaft Wrench from Murry Springs, Arizona." *Science*, January 12, 1968, 186–87.

Krause, Richard A. "Archeology of the Midwest." *Science*, April 17, 1987, 339–40.

MacDonald, George F. "Eastern North America." In *Early Man in the New World*, 97–108. Beverly Hills, California: Sage Publications, 1983.

"Man May Have Been in America for 36,000 Years." *Tulsa World*, May 3, 1991.

Morgan, Andy. "Vacation Digs." *Oklahoma Today,* March/April 1990, 29–35.

Niederberger, Christine. "Early Sedentary Economy in the Basin of Mexico." *Science,* January 12, 1979, 131–42.

Reagan, Michael J., and others. "Flake Tools Stratified Below Paleo-Indian Artifacts." *Science,* June 16, 1978, 1272–74.

Stanford, Dennis. "The Ginsberg Experiment." *Natural History,* September 1987, 10–14.

5.   The Big Game Hunters

Barse, William P. "Preceramic Occupation in Orinoco River Valley." *Science,* December 7, 1990, 1388–90.

Bartlett, Alexandra S., Elso S. Barghoorn, and Rainer Berger. "Fossil Maize from Panama." *Science,* July 25, 1969, 384–90.

Bower, B. "Promising New Clues to Early Americans." *Science News,* April 23, 1988, 261.

Bryan, Alan L. "Points of Order." *Natural History,* June 1987, 6–11.

Carlson, Roy L. "The Far West." In *Early Man in the New World,* 73–96. Beverly Hills, California: Sage Publications, 1983.

Carr, Robert S. "Early Man in South Florida." *Archaeology,* November/December 1987, 62–63.

Dumond, Don E. "The Archeology of Alaska and the Peopling of America." *Science,* August 29, 1980, 984–91.

Fagan, Brian M. *The Great Journey: The Peopling of Ancient America.* New York: Thames and Hudson, 1987.

Fairbridge, Rhodes W. "Shellfish-Eating Preceramic Indians in Coastal Brazil." *Science,* January 30, 1976, 353–59.

Gallant, Roy A. "Who Were the First Americans?" *Science 81,* April 1981, 94–96.

Gramly, R. Michael. "The First New Englanders." *Archaeology,* May/June 1988, 48–49.

Grayson, Donald K. "Death by Natural Causes." *Natural History,* May 1987, 8–12.

Griffin, James B. "The Origin and Dispersion of American Indians in North America." In *The First Americans: Origins, Affinities, and Adaptations,* 43–45. New York: Gustav Fischer, 1979.

Haynes, C. Vance, Jr. "The Earliest Americans." *Science,* November 7, 1969, 709–15.

Kirk, Ruth. "The Discovery of Marmes Man." *Natural History,* December 1968, 56–59.

Lahren, Larry, and Robson Bonnichsen. "Bone Foreshafts from a Clovis Burial in Southwestern Montana." *Science,* October 11, 1974, 147–50.

Lewin, Roger. "The First Americans Are Getting Younger." *Science,* November 27, 1987, 1230–32.

———. "Domino Effect Invoked in Ice Age Extinctions." *Science,* December 11, 1987, 1509–10.

Luckenback, Alvin, C. G. Holland, and Ralph C. Allen. "Soapstone Artifacts: Tracing Prehistoric Trade Patterns in Virginia." *Science,* January 10, 1975, 57–58.

MacNeish, Richard S. "Mesoamerica." In *Readings from Scientific American: New World Archaeology,* 125–36. San Francisco: W. H. Freeman and Company, 1974.

Marshall, Eliot. "Clovis Counterrevolution." *Science,* August 17, 1990, 738–41.

Martin, Paul S. "Clovisia the Beautiful!" *Natural History,* October 1987, 10–13.

McMillan, R. Bruce. "Early Canid Burial from the Western Ozark Highland." *Science,* February 27, 1970, 1246–47.

Mehringer, Peter J., Jr. "Clovis Cache Found — Weapons of Ancient Americans." *National Geographic,* October 1988, 500–503.

Miller, Carl F. "Russel Cave: New Light on Stone Age Life." *National Geographic,* March 1958, 427–36.

Schwartz, Douglas W. "Prehistoric Man in Mammoth Cave." *Scientific American,* July 1960, 130–40.

Shutler, Richard, Jr. *Early Man in the New World.* Beverly Hills, California: Sage Publications, 1983.

Skow, John. "This Florida Spa Holds a Surprising Lode of Prehistory." *Smithsonian,* December 1986, 72–78.

Wagner, Erika, and Carlos Schubert. "Pre-Hispanic Workshop of Serpentinite Artifacts, Venezuelan Andes, and Possible Raw Material Source." *Science,* February 22, 1972, 888–90.

Wedel, Waldo R. "Salvage Archaeology in the Missouri River Basin." *Science,* May 5, 1967, 589–97.

Zevallos M., Carlos, and others. "The San Pablo Corn Kernel and Its Friends." *Science,* April 22, 1977, 385–89.

6.   The Beginnings of Civilization

Adovasio, J. M., and Ronald C. Carlisle. "Pennsylvania Pioneers." *Natural History,* December 1986, 20–27.

Aldenderfer, Mark. "Middle Archaic Period Domestic Architecture from Southern Peru." *Science,* September 30, 1988, 1828–30.

Allman, William F., and Joannie M. Schrof. "Lost Empires of the Americas." *U. S. News and World Report,* April 2, 1990, 46–54.

Bawden, Garth L. "A Long Line of Brilliant Societies." *Archaeology,* May/June 1989, 54–59.

Bower, B. "Domesticating an Ancient Temple Town." *Science News,* October 15, 1988, 246.

———. "Ancient City Shows Where Cotton Was King." *Science News,* January 19, 1991, 38.

Bradbury, J. Platt. "Late Quaternary Environmental History of Lake Valencia, Venezuela." *Science*, December 18, 1981, 1299–1305.

Bryan, Alan L. "Points of Order." *Natural History*, June 1987, 6–11.

Burger, Richard L. "Long Before the Inca." *Natural History*, February 1989, 66–72.

Cobean, Robert H., and others. "Obsidian Trade at San Lorenzo Tenochtitlan, Mexico." *Science*, November 12, 1977, 666–71.

Costantin, M. M. "She Tells Us How They Lived." *Washington University Alumni Magazine*, Spring 1990, 14–19.

Euler, Robert C. "Willow Figurines from Arizona." *Natural History*, March 1966, 62–66.

Euler, Robert C., and others. "The Colorado Plateaus: Cultural Dynamics and Paleoenvironment." *Science*, September 14, 1979, 1089–1101.

Fasquelle, Ricardo A., and William Fash, Jr. "Copan: A Royal Maya Tomb Discovered." *National Geographic*, October 1989, 481–87.

Frison, George C. "The Western Plains and Mountain Region." In *Early Man in the New World*, 109–24. Beverly Hills, California: Sage Publications, 1973.

Gallant, Roy A. "Who Were the First Americans?" *Science 81*, April 1981, 94–96.

Gibbons, Ann. "New View of Early Amazonia." *Science*, June 22, 1990, 1488–90.

Gilbert, Susan. "Lost Cities of the Andes." *Science Digest*, June 1985, 46–53.

Griffin, James B. "The Origin and Dispersion of American Indians in North America." In *The First Americans: Origins, Affinities, and Adaptations*, 43–55. New York: Gustav Fischer, 1979.

Hammond, Norman. "The Earliest Maya." *Scientific American*, March 1977, 116–33.

Heizer, Robert F., and Lewis K. Napton. "Biological and Cultural Evidence from Prehistoric Human Coprolites." *Science*, September 8, 1969, 563–64.

Kaplan, L., Thomas F. Lynch, and C. E. Smith, Jr. "Early Cultivated Beans (*Phaseolus Vulgaris*) from an Intermontane Peruvian Valley." *Science*, January 5, 1973, 76–77.

Krause, Richard A. "Archeology of the Midwest." *Science*, April 17, 1987, 339–40.

Levathes, Louis E. "Peat Holds Clues to Early American Life." *National Geographic*, March 1987, 406–7.

Linares, Olga F., Payson D. Sheets, and E. Jane Rosenthal. "Prehistorical Agriculture in Tropical Highlands." *Science*, January 17, 1975, 137–45.

MacNeish, Richard S. "Early Man in the Andes." In *Readings from Scientific American: New World Archaeology*, 143–55. San Francisco: W. H. Freeman and Company, 1974.

Marcus, Joyce. "First Dates." *Natural History*, April 1991, 26–37.

Mazur, Suzan. "Visions of the Alto Magdalena." *Archaeology*, November/December 1989, 28–35.

"Mummy Autopsies." *Science Digest*, December 1981, 97.

Niederberger, Christine. "Early Sedentary Economy in the Basin of Mexico." *Science*, January 122, 1979, 131–42.

Pfeiffer, John E. "The Mysterious Rise and Decline of Monte Alban." *Smithsonian*, February 1980, 62–74.

Pires-Ferreira, Jane Wheeler, and Edgardo Pires-Ferreira. "Preceramic Animal Utilization in the Central Peruvian Andes." *Science*, October 29, 1976, 483–90.

Reeves, B. O. K. "Six Millenniums of Buffalo Kills," *Scientific American*, October 1983, 120–35.

Rensberger, Boyce. "Black Kings of Ancient America." *Science Digest*, September 1981, 74–78.

Roosevelt, Anna. "Lost Civilizations of the Lower Amazon." *Natural History*, February 1989, 74–83.

Schwartz, Douglas W. "Prehistoric Man in Mammoth Cave." *Scientific American*, July 1960, 130–40.

Sjoberg, Gideon. "The Origin and Evolution of Cities." In *Readings from Scientific American: New World Archaeology*, 271–80. San Francisco: W. H. Freeman and Company, 1974.

Skow, John. "This Florida Spa Holds a Surprising Lode of Prehistory." *Smithsonian*, December 1986, 72–78.

Smith, Bruce D. "Origins of Agriculture in Eastern North America." *Science*, December 1989, 1566–71.

Smith, Gary. "Secrets of the Mummies." *Discover*, October 1986, 72–81.

Snow, Dean. "The Changing Prey of Maine's Early Hunters." *Natural History*, November 1974, 15–22.

Stuart, George E. "City of Kings and Commoners." *National Geographic*, October 1989, 488–504.

Tuck, James A., and Robert J. McGhee. "An Archaic Indian Burial Mound in Labrador." *Scientific American*, November 1976, 122–29.

Turpin, Solveig. "Rock Art of the Despoblado." *Archaeology*, September/October 1988, 50–55.

Zeitlin, Robert N. "An Ancient Sacred Center." *Science*, July 1, 1988, 103–4.

7. The Rise of Empires and Nations

Adams, Richard E. W. "Rio Azul." *National Geographic*, April 1986, 420–50.

Allman, William, and Joanie M. Schrof. "Lost Empires of the Americas." *U. S. News and World Report*, April 2, 1990, 46–54.

Alva, Walter. "Discovering the New World's Richest Unlooted Tomb." *National Geographic*, October 1988, 510–22.

———. "The Moche of Ancient Peru." *National Geographic,* June 1990, 2–16.

"Arthritic Origins in New World?" *Science News,* April 2, 1988, 232.

Aveni, Anthony F. "The Nazca Lines: Patterns in the Desert." *Archaeology,* July/August 1986, 33–39.

Bower, B. "Grave Findings at Ancient Mexican Site." *Science News,* December 17, 1988, 388.

———. "Water Storage Spurred Growth of Maya Cities." *Science News,* February 9, 1991, 85.

Browman, David, "Palace in the Clouds." *Washington University Alumni Magazine,* Fall 1984, 9–16.

Carlson, John B. "America's Ancient Skywatchers." *National Geographic,* March 1990, 76–107.

Chen, Allan. "Unraveling Another Mayan Mystery." *Discover,* June 1987, 40–49.

Cobean, Robert H., and others. "Obsidian Trade at San Lorenzo Tenochtitlan, Mexico." *Science,* November 12, 1977, 666–71.

Colligan, Douglas. "Mayan Astronomy, Science of a Super Civilization." *Science Digest,* February 1974, 10–15.

Culbert, T. Patrick. "The Maya Enter History." *Natural History,* April 1985, 42–48.

Denevan, William M. "Aboriginal Drained-Field Agriculture in the Americas." *Science,* August 14, 1970, 647–54.

"Did Tectonics Topple the Chimu?" *Science News,* March 1983, 25.

Donnan, Christopher B. "Masterworks of Art Reveal a Remarkable Pre-Inca World." *National Geographic,* June 1990, 17–33.

Dorfman, Andrea. "Demystifying the Maya." *Science Digest,* September 1984, 26.

Epstein, Nadine. "From a Remote Jungle Site, a Trail of Striking Clues." *Smithsonian,* December 1989, 98–113.

Fagan, Brian M. *The Great Journey: The Peopling of Ancient America.* New York: Thames and Hudson, 1978.

Fash, William L., Jr., and Barbara W. Fash. "Scribes, Warriors, and Kings: The Lives of the Copan Maya." *Archaeology,* May/June 1990, 26–29.

Fasquelle, Ricardo Agurcia. "Copan: A Royal Maya Tomb Discovered" *National Geographic,* October 1989, 418–87.

Flagg, Mary Jo. "Dig We Must! Such a Slogan Fated a Mayan Empire to Dust." *Science Digest,* October 1978, 77–79.

Folan, William J., Laraine A. Fletcher, and Ellen Kintz. "Fruit, Fiber, Bark, and Resin: Social Organization of a Maya Urban Center." *Science,* May 18, 1979, 679–700.

Freidel, David. "A Mesoamerican Middle Age." *Science,* July 6, 1990, 78–79.

Gallant, Roy A. *Ancient Indians: The First Americans.* Hillside New Jersey: Enslow Publishers, 1989.

Garret, Wilbur E. "LaRuta Maya." *National Geographic,* October 1989, 424–79.

Grove, David. "A Mesoamerican Culture." *Science,* April 15, 1981, 808–10.

Hammond, Norman. "Unearthing the Oldest Known Maya." *National Geographic,* July 1982, 126–40.

———. "The Exploration of the Maya World." *American Scientist,* September/October 1982, 482–95.

———. "The Discovery of Tikal." *Archaeology,* May/June 1987, 30–37.

Hathaway, Bruce. "The Ancient Canal That Turned Uphill." *Science 82,* October 1982, 80–81.

Healy, Paul F. "Music of the Maya." *Archaeology,* January/February 1988, 24–31.

Isbell, William H., and Anita G. Cook. "Ideological Origins of an Andean Conquest State." *Archaeology,* July/August 1987, 27–33.

Kolata, Alan L. "Tiwanaku and Its Hinterland." *Archaeology,* January/February 1987, 36–41.

Malmstrom, Vincent H. "Where Time Began." *Science Digest,* December 1981, 56–113.

McIntyre, Loren. "Mystery of the Ancient Nazca Lines." *National Geographic,* May 1975, 716–28.

Morris, Craig. "Master Design of the Inca." *Natural History,* December 1976, 57–67.

———. "A City Fit for an Inka." *Archaeology,* September/October 1988, 43–49.

"Pollen Proof of Early Maya Farming." *Science News,* April 4, 1987, 218.

Scarborough., V. L., and G. G. Gallopin. "A Water Storage Adaptation in the Maya Lowlands." *Science,* February 8, 1991.

Schaedel, Richard. "The Lost Cities of Peru." In *Readings from Scientific American: New World Archaeology,* 26–32. San Francisco: W. H. Freeman and Company, 1974.

Smith, Bruce, D. "*Chenopodium* as a Prehistoric Domesticate in Eastern North America: Evidence from Russell Cave, Alabama." *Science,* October 1984, 165–67.

Turner, B. L., II. "Prehistoric Intensive Agriculture in Mayan Lowlands." *Science,* July 12, 1974, 118–23.

Von Hagen, Victor W. "America's Oldest Roads." In *Readings from Scientific American: New World Archaeology,* 33–36. San Francisco: W. H. Freeman and Company, 1974.

Wilkerson, Jeffrey K. "Man's Eighty Centuries in Veracruz." *National Geographic,* August 1980, 203–31.

8.   The Rise of Nations in the United States

Adams, Daniel B. "Last Ditch Archeology." *Science 83,* December 1983, 28–37.

"Anasazi Astronomers." *Science Digest,* May 1983, 24.

Bassett, Carol Ann. "The Sun of the Anasazi." *Science 85,* September, 1985, 86–87.

Brian, Jeffrey P. "The Great Mound Robbery." *Archaeology,* May/June 1988, 18–25.

Carlson, John B. "America's Ancient Skywatchers." *National Geographic,* March 1990, 76–107.

Diamond, Jared. "The Golden Age That Never Was." *Discover,* December 1988, 78–79.

———. "The Accidental Conqueror." *Discover,* December 1989, 71–76.

Fagan, Brian M. *The Great Journey: The Peopling of Ancient America.* New York: Thames and Hudson, 1987.

Faulkner, Charles H. "Painters of the Dark Zone." *Archaeology,* March/April 1988, 30–38.

Fiedel, Stuart J. *Prehistory of the Americas.* New York: Cambridge University Press, 1987.

Folsom, Franklin. "Mysterious Mounds at Poverty Point." *Science Digest,* February 1972, 46–54.

Fowler, Melvin L., ed. *Explorations into Cahokia Archaeology.* Urbana, Illinois: Illinois Archaeological Survey, 1973.

Gallant, Roy A. "Who Were the First Americans?" *Science 81,* April 1981, 94–96.

Grant, Campbell. "California's Legacy of Indian Rock Art." *Natural History,* June/July 1964, 32–41

Griffin, Gillett G. "In Defense of the Collector." *National Geographic,* April 1986, 462–65.

Hecht, Robert A. "Anasazi Trails." *Archaeology,* May/June 1987, 22–29.

Hirschfeld, Carson. "Sacred Places." *Archaeology,* January/February 1990, 42–49.

Iseminger, William R. "Excavations at Cahokia Mounds." *Archaeology,* January/February 1986, 58–59.

Keith, Sandra., "Ancient Ones." *Friendly Exchange,* August 1987, 10–16.

Lekson, Stephen. "Chaco Canyon, New Mexico." *Archaeology,* May/June 1987, 22–29.

Lobdell, John E. "An Eagle Eye." *Archaeology,* November/December 1989, 48–53.

Martin, Paul S. "The Peoples of Pine Lawn Valley," in *Readings from Scientific American: New World Archaeology,* 171–75. San Francisco: W. H. Freeman and Company, 1974.

Masse, W. Bruce. "Prehistoric Irrigation Systems in the Salt River Valley, Arizona." *Science,* October 28, 1981, 408–15.

McAdams, William. *Records of Ancient Races in the Mississippi Valley.* St. Louis: C. R. Barnes Publishing Co., 1887.

Meighan, Clement W. "Prehistory of West Mexico." *Science,* June 21, 1974, 1254–61.

Palca, Joseph. "Sun Dagger Misses Its Mark." *Science,* June 30, 1989, 1538.

Pastron, Allen G. "Surprise Shellmound." *Archaeology,* January/February 1990, 16.

Prufer, Olaf H. "The Hopewell Cult." In *Readings from Scientific American: New World Archaeology.* San Francisco: W. H. Freeman and Company, 1974.

Reyman, Jonathan E. "An Anasazi Solar Marker?" *Science,* August 22, 1980, 858–60.

Shafer, Harry J. "Excavating the Nan Ruin." *Archaeology,* November/December 1990, 49–51.

Silverberg, Robert. *Mound Builders of America: The Archaeology of a Myth.* Greenwich, Connecticut: New York Graphic Society, 1968.

Smith, Gary, and Michael E. Long. "Utah's Rock Art Wilderness Louvre." *National Geographic,* January 1980, 97–117.

Sofar, Anna, Volker Zinser, and Rolf M. Sinclair. "A Unique Solar Marking Construct." *Science,* October 19, 1979, 283–91.

Stuart, George E. "Who Were the Mound Builders?" *National Geographic,* December 1972, 783–801.

"A Supernova Story in Clay." *Science News,* June 23, 1990, 396.

Wilford, John Noble. "Archaeologists in Arizona Discover 800-Year-Old Indian Catacombs." *The New York Times,* April 27, 1991.

Williamson, Ray. "Native Americans Were Continent's First Astronomers." *Smithsonian,* October 1978, 78–85.

Index

ABOUT THE AUTHOR AND ILLUSTRATOR

HELEN RONEY SATTLER taught elementary school and was a children's librarian before beginning her writing career with stories for her children. She is the respected author of more than thirty natural history books for children, including the award-winning *Hominids: A Look Back at Our Ancestors; Dinosaurs of North America* and *The Illustrated Dinosaur Dictionary; Baby Dinosaurs; Sharks, the Super Fish;* and *The Book of Eagles.* Mrs. Sattler lived in Bartlesville, Oklahoma, until her death in 1992.

JEAN DAY ZALLINGER previously collaborated with Helen Roney Sattler on *Baby Dinosaurs, Sharks,* and *The Book of Eagles.* She has illustrated more than fifty books for children, most of them about scientific subjects. Ms. Zallinger teaches illustration and drawing at the Paier College of Art. She lives in North Haven, Connecticut.